The King's Community, a personal view

The King's Community, a personal view

ALAN MACFARLANE

2019

First published in Great Britain
by Cam Rivers Publishing Ltd
2019

Devised by Zilan Wang
Written by Alan Macfarlane
Typesetting and layout design by Jaimie Norman
Marketing Manager James O'Sullivan

This publication has been generously supported by the Kaifeng Foundation.

Printed and Bound in Great Britain.

ISBN 978-1-798125-67-0

www.cambridgerivers.com
press@cambridgerivers.com

Contents

Preface: An historical anthropology of an unusual institution

I AM A social anthropologist and historian. As an anthropologist, I usually go to distant lands, to Nepal, Japan, China for example, and study a different way of life through participating and observing. I write about all aspects of the culture, economy, politics and religion of small or large communities.

When I came to the end of my Ordinary Professorial Fellowship at King's College in 2009, after being in the College for thirty-eight years, I realised that one of my longest and most intense pieces of fieldwork in a bounded community was in King's.

It had taken me some years to start to understand how this ancient foundation, more than five hundred years old, worked. I had learnt it through participating in teaching and administering, and also through doing dozens of interviews of those who had been students or taught in the College.

It seemed a waste not to gather together my impressions and understanding of how the College works as a community and present it to future historians or others who are interested.

I am aware that this is a portrait of something that has already changed greatly since I retired, though I am still a Life Fellow. King's today is different for both students and staff. So I am, as many anthropologists do, using the historical present tense about something that has partially vanished.

This is not a guide to King's, nor is it any kind of official introduction to the College. It is the view of an elderly, white, male, middle-class Englishman about the place in which he has had the privilege to be a member for nearly fifty years. Yet it may be of interest as a portrait of something unique and uniquely English, one of the most beautiful and distinguished Colleges in the world. There is no other account like this written from the inside but also with the tools of social anthropology as a comparative discipline.

I hope you will enjoy this little book, even while realising that it is as much a historical account of a disappearing world as any account of remote villages in the Amazon or the Himalayas.

I have taught many students from non-British backgrounds who find the cultural rules of the British, and particularly in the academic world, confusing. So I wrote down some guidelines for my students. I also found that many of my students and colleagues found the competing pressures of academic life overwhelming. So, I also wrote down a little of what I had learnt about time-management. I reproduce these two small bits of guidance at the end of this little book.

The King's Community

COMING TO KING'S for some days, weeks or years in the College is not easy. The College looks just like a large set of buildings in a modern city, an expensive hotel perhaps. Yet its long history of nearly 580 years (founded in 1441), and strange traditions, and the intensity of the termly rush makes it different. Not many have experienced such an overlapping of the physical, social, economic, political and spiritual worlds within a bounded community outside their home. I was trained for such an experience over the ten years of boarding schools. Most who now come to the College do not have such a preparation. A few notes on some of the features of this unusual place may be helpful.

Yet I am fully aware that everyone experiences a different King's, so my own account has to be personal. This is *my* King's. If I had written it at another time, I had been in a different discipline, a woman, from another class or ethnicity, I would describe it differently. Readers must adjust for the white, middle class, male, historical-anthropologist, born in Assam, India, in 1941.

What is King's?

If Cambridge and Oxford are strange this is clearly because of their unique collegiate structure. Like many things – happiness, love, beauty – it is true of Colleges that it is only when we try to define and describe the inner essence of something which we have often spoken about but never seriously analysed, that we realize that their meaning is elusive. The outward forms are obvious, the chapels, lawns, libraries, halls and the inhabitants are material enough. Yet when a perplexed new student or visitor to Cambridge asks me to explain what Colleges have been and are, I realize that I have lived within them without really understanding them.

People have often described the Colleges as little 'tribes' and the whole of the place as tribal. There are indeed some analogies. Like certain tribes, there is very little formally instituted leadership – the Head of House (a Provost in King's, Rector, Dean, Master etc. in other Colleges) has no

2

police force or taxation system to keep his or her Fellows[1] and students in place. There is often feuding both within and between Colleges, as there is between tribes. The Colleges have a corporate[2] structure similar to many tribes. Tribal 'property' - animals and other goods - is paralleled by corporate property in a College, that is in the wine, books, buildings and lawns. Both tribes and Colleges are perpetual bodies in which the members feel part of something larger than themselves.

Yet we immediately notice some profound differences. For example, although some tribal societies have dormitories and eating halls where they may keep their trophies, these only partly resemble the large dining hall with portraits, the Chapel, library and courtyards of King's.

To find more satisfactory analogies to the College, one needs to move to a different level. For the Colleges now exist within a civilization which in other ways is largely industrialized and individualistic, with few such integrated communities of living, learning and worshipping. The continued presence of Oxbridge Colleges feels increasingly anomalous, like a theme park or self-conscious drama. King's might have not felt strange to the English during the first five hundred years of its existence. Now it puzzles even the most astute observers.

How can such a community continue to exist alongside a modern, capitalist, industrial, individualist and technologically sophisticated civilization, and yet retain its distinctive 'otherness'? And what is this strange anomalous institution which does not fit into the categories of most of those who come here, particularly the large majority who have not come from boarding schools?

The heart of King's

King's is like the computers which were, to a considerable extent, dreamt of and devised in King's. It thinks, adapts, and changes with the world. Yet the programs which run it are often, in essence, centuries old. They were laid down early, but were general and flexible enough to absorb the vast transformation that would happen during its five-hundred and eighty-year history.

1   The meaning of terms used in this book such as 'Fellows', as well as some other Cambridge words with special meanings, are given at the glossary at the end of the book.
2   A corporation, from the latin for 'body', is an enduring entity, where individuals form part of a long-term whole.

Like the Ship of the Argonauts on its long voyage, King's has constantly had to be patched, bits replaced because rotten, new bits added for further journeys. Yet it is recognizably the same, in the way that a venerable old oak tree of more than half a millenium of continuous growth is still in many ways the little oak sapling of its youth. What King's stands for, its largely unstated goals which can never be captured in a 'mission statement', and the customs which can never be adequately described, is a set of practices and assumptions which have not fundamentally altered.

King's, as I have known it, stands for curiosity, openness, fellowship, wonder, humour, playfulness, awe, delight, argument, competitiveness, modesty, subversion, ceremonial, kindness, tolerance, beauty, utility, liberty, conformity and a whole bundle of often colliding and clashing values. Those who have navigated its still pools and rapids are attracted to many of these features in differing times and to different degrees.

Combined with its charm and a feeling of otherworldly magic, it seldom fails to make a deep impression, even if a person appears to forget or reject it. Like any powerful parent, it affects the rest of their lives, whether they like it or not. It evokes strong emotions.

Above all, this gives me, and many, a sense of hope. Here is a place which has preserved a set of ideals within beautiful surroundings for over half a millennium. Much of the treasure it has accumulated is not in its physical buildings, but in what the Japanese would describe as 'living national treasures'. The poets, scientists, philosophers and others, dead or alive, are its greatest gift, along with the large number of students who have passed through it and gone on to their diverse careers.

Alongside them are the cultural treasures, a set of manners, assumptions, and attitudes to life, which are not visible to the casual visitor. A tour of the College and the University, noting a few pictures and statues, or a walk along the Backs will give a visitor a sense that much must lie beneath this surface. What lies deeper is the hidden culture and history of a Royal College which has been one of the bridges into our twenty-first century world.

Communal resources and community

One of the striking features of an Oxbridge College, inherited from the multiple spaces of a medieval monastery, is the rich array of 'public' (in the sense of being freely available to a certain category of members of a College) spaces. I had assumed that such resources were natural in a place of higher education when I experienced them in my Oxford College, and then again through my years in Cambridge. Yet the intervening period at two London institutions (London School of Economics and then the School of Oriental and African Studies) and then visits to universities in other countries, especially spells as Visiting Professor at the top Japanese (Tokyo) and Chinese (Tsinghua) universities have made me realize that, in fact, this is very unusual. Most students and staff at British universities, let alone in China, Japan or elsewhere, have hardly any of the facilities I describe below.

It is worth considering why they exist only in Oxford and Cambridge. One obvious factor is the wealth of Colleges. Many universities could not afford to provide such amenities. Yet it is more than this. For example, Tsinghua or Tokyo universities have great wealth now and are constantly putting up very expensive new buildings. The same is true of some British universities. They choose to build teaching and research buildings and do not put aside any money for improved communal facilities outside the strictly academic sphere. Providing such communal resources is clearly not thought of as a high priority.

It might be thought that this is just a matter of preference. In fact, it is a political choice. In many parts of the world it would be considered dangerous to encourage too much space and time for students and staff to discuss, argue, question, perhaps associate and even 'plot'. So public spaces are largely restricted to teaching and research. Yet while this is certainly true in many parts of the world, the fact that most British universities are also very meagre in their provision of public facilities suggests that there are further reasons.

One might think that the provision of such spaces is related to the peculiarity in English law, which envisages the possibility of complex 'commons'. That is to say resources which are shared between individuals but which are neither fully private, nor fully public. This intermediary category is central to the idea of Trusts and English Common Law, but is not a category traditionally recognized in any other legal system in the world outside the area based on English law. When present, it means that you can have a field, house, library or church, which is shared by a sub-set of people, and which they can use in different ways, but is neither open to everyone automatically, nor the private property of an individual.

This peculiar feature of English law – giving the country its public libraries, parks, rights of way, schools, clubs – allows the phenomenon of communal resources to flourish. This may be a necessary, but not a sufficient, reason, for it would apply all over England and to a considerable extent Scotland. Yet, as noted, only Oxford and Cambridge Colleges, and the Inns of Court, have made use of this legal right to provide the facilities I am describing. So, there must be an added factor.

Here we come back to the fact that Oxford and Cambridge have preserved a system derived from medieval monastic organizations. Medieval monasteries were 'total' institutions - they had their church, library, gardens, dining space, dormitories and workshops. They catered for all parts of the lives of their single-sex members. This system has continued in Oxbridge Colleges, which see their role as places which provide for the spirit, heart and body as well as the mind. The resources can be seen as an expression (like other symbols such as crests, flags, scarfs, mottoes) of the existence of a community of Fellows and Scholars. They come for intense periods into an overlapping space, and actively share resources which support, and indeed construct, a sense of community.

The College, based on a monastery, was a place for the Spirit, a place of worship. Hence the importance of the Chapel. This is a space for all members of the College, and the wider public at particular times. It is open to all members of the College, but there is an internal division within it, as with some other resources. The Fellows have special seats – the great wooden stalls behind the Choir – the Provost and Vice Provost have even more special seats with their backs to the wooden screen. The Fellows also have the privilege of a number of free tickets to concerts and particularly to the varied Carol Services at Christmas. They can also go, with their guests, up onto the roof of the Chapel.

A second important communal space in a medieval monastery was the eating hall or refectory. Again, in King's, this, with its attendant cafeteria and kitchens, are open to all members of the College alike. Yet again there are internal divisions. The students pay a subsidised amount for their meals, while the Fellows get free meals. For many centuries, the Fellows sat apart at a raised or 'High' table, though this has partially been removed in the last forty years in King's. The table is not raised, but it is reserved for the Fellows at dinner.

While the Fellows are not set apart by a High Table, they have preserved a separate room to which they can retire on two or three nights a week during term. This is called the Wine Room, and is furnished with a long table around which is passed the port, claret, fruit, cheese etc. Snuff was still present when I first came to King's and the atmosphere is enhanced by the portraits of distinguished ancestors on the walls. It is served from the Pantry, which is also mainly for Fellows and their guests, where they can buy wine, or order sandwiches for lunch.

There is also a private set of dining and entertainment rooms, known as the Saltmarsh rooms. The rooms are filled with Bloomsbury period paintings by Roger Fry and Duncan Grant. It is here, for instance, that I held my wedding reception, launch parties for a couple of books, and farewell party when I ended my time as a Professor in the University.

A third important space in a monastic community was the library. King's has an important library (with over 130,000 books) which dates back to its founding, though it has been housed in different locations, including parts of the Chapel. It is open to students 24/7, and has internet access to other libraries. There is also the associated Archive Centre, where important collections of papers (Keynes, Forster, Leach) are kept. There is also the Rowe Music Library which has a fine collection of recordings.

The fourth important set of spaces is the living accommodation. There are many rooms within the College in the various buildings, most of them occupied by the students who will have a bed, desk, and access to cooking and washing facilities. These are the relics of medieval monastic cells. Again, there is a hierarchy. The Fellows, depending on their needs and status, will have access to bigger rooms and, in the past, to small flats, including one or two which still exist in the College, in which they lived (with a living room, bedroom, study and access to some cooking and washing facilities).

With the growth of the College, there is not room now on the main site for all of the students, and particularly the married graduate students. So there are a number of undergraduate and graduate hostels, most of them on College grounds either across the street from the College, or in the College grounds. Among them are rooms in Tennis Court Road, Grasshopper Lodge, Cranmer Road, King's Parade and Kingsfield. There is a coin-operated laundry on the main College site and in most hostels, trunk rooms for students to store their possessions during vacations, bicycle racks both underground and above ground.

Then there are the spaces for walking, running, playing games and water sports. All members of the College can walk around the extensive grounds through to the back gate, but only the Senior Members can walk on the grass (though in the summer the students hold various events on the lawns).

All members can book the College punts, canoes and kayaks. There is a boat house down the Cam belonging to the College, from which two men's and two women's boating crews operate. There are also playing fields (shared with Selwyn College), with rugby, football, hockey and cricket pitches and several grass tennis courts. King's students can also use the hard surface tennis courts and squash courts at King's College School. There is also a multigym, with cardio vascular and resistance equipment, as well as some weights and a stretching area, as well as a separate Freeweights Gym.

There are several facilities for seminars, talks and lectures - available to be booked by all members of the College. There is a big room called the Chetwynd Room (with a large open-air courtyard attached), and beyond that a lecture hall named after John Maynard Keynes. There is a room named after Donald Beves for seminars or an overflow eating room from the Hall. There is an elegant seminar room in the old lodge where the Accounts office used to be.

There is an Art Centre, available for teaching and exhibitions, and also a Dark Room, with chemicals and equipment for processing negatives and printmaking. There are two Steinway pianos available for student use and two music practice rooms in the grounds and further practice rooms nearby in the King's School. There is a computer room, named after Alan Turing, with computers available to students 24/7, as well as a card-operated photocopier. There is a TV room on the main site, and also TVs in common rooms in several of the hostels. The King's College Student Union (KCSU) and King's College Graduate Society (KCGS) have a collection of more than 130 films for students to borrow, as well as a collection of comic books.

There is the King's Bar, with a pool table, quiz machine, table football and daily newspapers. Drinks are available at lunch and in the evening and events are organised here. Next to it is the King's Coffee Shop, which serves snacks and drinks through the day. And below it is the 'Bunker', an area for parties, gymnastics and yoga. The Graduate Suite overlooks the main King's courtyard. It includes a study, graduate computer room, and a reading room, as well as coffee and tea making facilities.

There is a Fellows' Garden, an important, beautifully preserved, nineteenth-century style garden with a varied set of trees and plants sent back by Fellows from all over the world. According to the College website 'Students can use the large, picturesque Fellows' Garden at any time'. This is a popular spot in the warmer weather for a break with friends, a pretty place to study and for garden parties. There is also a croquet lawn. It is used for various events, particularly in the summer when it is open to the public for certain days for charity, used for plays (especially Shakespeare), concerts, poetry readings and for parties to celebrate the end of examinations. It is mirrored by a smaller, Chinese-style, garden, the Xu Zhimo Friendship Garden beside the King's bridge.

There are a number of allotments where students can grow food. These are looked after by the college gardeners during the vacations. Students use the private west bank (the other side of the Cam) with a wonderful view of the College, as well as the private Bodley's court lawn and benches for sitting and reading.

Finally, at the entrance to the College, the Porter's Lodge is a hub of the College. Each student has a pigeonhole there on one side of the entrance. The Fellows have their pigeonholes on the other side, and have the privilege of having their mail delivered daily to their rooms. The Porters are central to College life and the Head Porter is one of the most important members of the College.

It has been noted that Fellows have certain privileges within the communal facilities for worship, eating and drinking, walking and other aspects of life. They also have a certain area where students are not, except on special occasions, allowed.

The Senior Combination Room, is named thus because, among other things, it is where the Fellows 'combine' or come together before formal meals. In Oxford, these rooms are called the Senior Common Room. This important space is again inherited from the common meeting room which was a part of a medieval monastery, and then, after the Reformation, and particularly from the nineteenth century, it became a kind of club room. Its decor, chairs and tables, piled newspapers, portraits and customs echo many club rooms across British professional institutions - the army, law, church, business.

This is where Fellows can bring their guests before or after meals, or have relaxed but perhaps significant conversations with other Fellows. The motto of the room might well be taken from the motto of the

French Republic, liberty, equality and fraternity (or 'sorority' with many women Fellows nowadays). A new institution of 'Associates of the Senior Combination Room' has been introduced to recognize the work of a number of those who help the College in its daily work. It is a room where the Governing Body of the College meets.

Next to it is a small 'Orangery' where coffee and tea is permanently on hand, and off that a small Octagonal room which has portraits of the College and easy chairs, and where small meetings can be held, perhaps devising strategies before a formal public meeting. Through the adjacent buttery there are the steps down to the College Cellars. These are large and well stocked, and Fellows have the right to keep a certain amount of their own wine on certain shelves.

The Heads of Cambridge Colleges were allowed to marry from very early on in the history of Cambridge. In King's the Provost was particularly important, and was originally known as the Provost of Cambridge. So, the Master's or Provost's Lodge is usually a large building with dining room, drawing room and other entertainment rooms. The one in Trinity is particularly grand, but that in King's, spread between the Old and the newly built Lodge is quite spacious, with its own garden. Fellows, with the agreement of the Provost, can use some of these facilities for academic or entertainment purposes. Other special rooms (Rylands Rooms) in the Old Lodge can be booked for special guests and Fellows also have certain guest rooms, which they can book for visitors at a reasonable rate.

Finally, there are two particular resources of some importance. This is the right of parking, either for short periods on the forecourt outside the front gate of the College, or for longer in two car parks behind the Fellows garden.

Everything, of course, constantly changes, but the signs of communal life expand in certain places (for example in student facilities) while they shrink in other ways. For example, when I first came to the College there was communal shoe cleaning equipment and even a communal hair brush, as I recall, as well as a larger supply of communal gowns. And the College headed notepaper and cards on which one wrote angry letters to *The Times* have disappeared in the age of the internet.

A Working College

Fellowship

PART OF THE special essence of King's and other Colleges is the nature of Fellowship. 'Fellowship' denotes equality, friendship, closeness, but also (implicitly) a separate identity and dignity. It is a very English concept, as in the group of knights who fought for King Arthur, or hobbits and others who sought the Ring - the Fellowship of the Round Table, the Fellowship of the Ring. In a big College like King's there are many varieties of Fellowship - Senior and Junior, Life and Honorary, Official and Unofficial, but they are all Fellows and should treat each other not merely with respect but as instituted friends.

Fellowship generates sentiment, a feeling of closeness and being of one body, but, just like a family, it does not necessarily generate agreement. You don't necessarily like all the Fellows, just as you may not like some of your family. For many purposes, whatever your personal feelings, you feel some sense of respect, closeness and trust. When I recognize Fellows, I greet them. When I sit down next to one of them at a meal, I feel a sense of shared identity. This takes away a little of the isolation and separateness which is a strong feature of the individualistic English.

The secret, I suppose, is the feeling of a shared purpose. You are a team, but not one that is trying to score the most goals, or win a race, but together are trying to push forward the task you accepted in the oath you took when you joined the Fellowship. Jointly, you are trying to promote the College as a centre of 'education, religion, learning and research'.

It is this sense of shared task, ineffable yet rewarding, which sometimes spreads to others in longer-term contact with the College – porters, secretaries, gardeners – which helps to explain an anomaly. This is that while the written contractual obligations of a University teacher or Fellow are often almost non-existent, you find yourself doing many extra hours and tasks, beyond the limited call of duty derived from some diffused sense of obligation, debt, desire for approbation, or desire to reciprocate the perceived efforts of others.

Of course, there are a few 'free riders' and minimal participants, and there are times when people put in more effort than at others. Yet it is generally the case that a sense of privileged 'belonging', a desire to be thought of as worthy of the Fellowship, is a nebulous force which drives many on. The University and College become something like the Protestant idea of God – constantly there, watching, praising, encouraging and occasionally showing signs of disapproval at some failure or lack of effort.

The economic base

A College, in the legal sense of 'The Provost and Scholars', is an economic unit. It owns and administers property which has been given to it over the ages, including farms and houses, which it has sometimes developed over time into companies, factories and nowadays science parks and shopping malls. It also has intellectual property, for example the rights in television productions of E.M. Forster's books or J.M. Keynes' papers are owned by King's. The College itself consists of a series of buildings where the students live during term time and where Fellows teach. In King's these buildings are worth many millions of pounds, as are the fields and gardens and school. King's now also makes a considerable sum from conferences, and even more from the rising number of visitors to the College.

The staff who run what is, in effect, a small country estate, include a considerable number of cooks, serving staff, bedmakers, builders and repairers. There are also those who help on the intellectual and ceremonial side, including librarians, archivists and Chapel attendants. There are numerous other staff, including porters, secretaries and gardeners. These staff are in many ways the core of the College, and the Head Porter, Catering Manager, Head Gardener (Senior Horticulturalist nowadays) and others are very important in the College.

Because most Colleges are significant economic units, small businesses and property holders, they have various officials whose prime responsibility is managing this aspect of College affairs. The chief of these is the Bursar, who oversees the income and expenditure and inspects the properties, and, in King's, a Domus Bursar to look after the buildings. Various committees of Fellows, with names such as the Investment Committee and Inspectors of Accounts advise the Bursar and monitor the finances, which are regularly reported to the College Governing Body.

Governance

The Provost, Bursar, Domestic Bursar, Senior Tutor and Dean of Chapel form an inner circle of power, along with the Vice-Provost, who chairs some committees and is in charge of Fellows' social arrangements and rooms. These College Officers meet weekly along with a small number of Fellows and student representatives to oversee the day-to-day running of the College, especially the teaching side. They form the College Council, and nowadays are formally named as the Trustees of the charitable trust which the College is classified as. Their major decisions have to be approved by the whole Fellowship.

The Fellows meet twice a term as the 'Governing Body', a kind of Parliament. To underline the formality of the proceedings, gowns are worn, official titles are usually used, people stand up to make their points and communication is channeled through the Provost, who is in the Chair. Students attend the 'Open Business', but matters concerning specific members of the College or Staff are dealt with in 'Reserved Business'. On important and controversial issues a vote is taken by a show of hands and there are various complex rules as to what constitutes a sufficient majority.

Once a year there is a larger-scale meeting, the 'Annual Congregation', when all of the accounts are examined and elections to committees and Honorary Fellowships are dealt with and a special lunch is held where 'audit ale' is drunk. At King's, the Fellowship is divided into groups, sometimes by real or 'social age' – Senior, Middle, Junior - sometimes on some other principle. These have the quaint, Alice in Wonderland, name of 'Caucuses'. They meet to discuss items before the Annual Congregation and the membership of committees. They also meet to discuss particularly important events such as the election of a Provost or Vice-Provost.

There are many sub-parts of the College and these are directed by a formal head - Librarian, Senior Horticulturalist, Dean of Chapel, Director of Development and others. Each of these, and other functions of the College are dealt with by sub-committees who report to the Council and the Governing Body. Thus, there are committees for Finance, Wine, the Garden, the Library and the Chapel, and others for Adornments (paintings etc), Visitors, Catering, and to help raise money for the College, and to advise on the election of Fellows. The students have their own King's College Students' Union with a committee.

The Social World

College clubs and associations

THERE ARE MANY clubs in King's. Among those currently operating as clubs in 2018, are the following: the King's Drama Society which puts on plays; the King's Film Society; the King's allotments where students can grow vegetables, and an Apiculture society, which keeps bees; the King's College Music Society, ranging widely over different types of music; a mountaineering and kayaking society; a King's Politics group, to invite speakers and hold debates; the King's College Student Union (undergraduate), covering welfare, access, ethnic minorities, green and charities, international students, entertainment etc.; King's College Graduate Society which organizes many events; a number of subject societies including the King's Law Society, the Biology seminar series, the Maths and Physics society, the History Society. There are also many sporting groups and societies, in particular in relation to rowing and team games.

These clubs teach people how to organize and work together and often inspire a person to develop an interest which remains important for the rest of their life. Each club has its own peculiar characteristics in terms of when and where they meet and their local customs.

The present clubs are descendants of many earlier, often bizarre and sometimes influential societies. In King's there was one club which was formed by Lytton Strachey and Leonard Woolf (of Trinity), among others, called 'The Midnight Society' which met on 'K' staircase on Saturdays at midnight in Clive Bell's rooms, a precursor of the Bloomsbury Group. Another was the 'Political Economy Club' which was founded by John Maynard Keynes, with professors, graduate students and some undergraduates were members of.

One particularly intriguing society was the 'Cambridge Apostles', so-called because there were, at any one time, only twelve members, like Christ's apostles. It was particularly associated with Trinity and, in its later years, with King's. It was important because it was the apex of the Cambridge system. Other clubs and societies took people out into the wider world. The Apostles chose particularly promising undergraduates who looked as if they might turn into brilliant thinkers, writers and artists, some of whom would stay in Cambridge. It surrounded this process with secrecy and ritual. It was forbidden to talk about the membership or proceedings to others. It was something like a Masonic brotherhood and once a member, there were lifetime obligations of support and intimacy.

Young and old

Cambridge is both sage and filled with child-like enthusiasms. For most of their past, Oxford and Cambridge were boarding institutions for young boys who moved through their adolescence into early adulthood at university. It was here that the boy became the man. Through this 'rite of transition', a young person emerged ready for the world of adult responsibilities. It was often a period of freedom, of separation from the world in order to make it possible to re-enter it with a different status. The Colleges acted *in loco parentis*, in the place of parents.

This is such an obvious function of King's today that it is easy to miss it. There are rites of incorporation at the start, a period of liminality and licence with inculcation into new knowledge in the middle, and a rite of dis-aggregation at the end (degree ceremonies etc). This gives the basic structure to the undergraduate course. There is a first year of innocence, a second of gaining knowledge, a third of 'finals' which ties it all together before the nostalgically remembered 'Salad Days' are over.

This central feature of ritual and social transition is now partly concealed by the growing number of postgraduates and the movement of the age of undergraduates from 14-17 to 18-21 over the eighteenth and nineteenth centuries. Those who come up are already in many ways sophisticated and mature. Yet many are still on the cusp between adolescence and maturity and this gives Cambridge its special youthful feeling. Over half of the University population is aged 18-21, full of a mixture of innocence, nearness to childhood, enthusiasm, open futures, exploring minds. This seeps into the soul of even the crabbiest old don who each year partly relives his or her own years as a hopeful young monster.

The jokes, pranks, satires, spirited life of the bar, the disco, the Union, the clubs and societies are all related to this period of testing, trying and expanding. The hobbies and interests at school can now be broadened, the first solo journeys to foreign lands undertaken. New passions for ideas, and perhaps the first serious love affairs can blossom.

Play

Foreigners visiting Oxford and Cambridge in the nineteenth century were amazed at the huge emphasis on competitive games and sports in the life of the two Universities. The 'boat race between Oxford and Cambridge and the inter-university cricket matches had already begun as early as 1827, and became annual events in 1839.'[3] Boat clubs and other athletic organizations and inter-collegiate competitions became a well-established feature of the University. The emphasis on sports was a continuation of what was happening in the public schools and helped to bridge the transition from school to university.

The Cambridge University Diary includes the year's almanac, examination timetable, university officers, libraries, museums, Colleges and other matters in a few pages. It then devotes two pages to 'The River' with the 'Order of Boats in the Main Division'. Then a further two pages are given to 'Inter-University' contests, one third of which are 'Women's Matches'. There are 13 'Full Blue' sports, and another 26 'Discretionary' and 'Half Blue Sports', including Judo, Karate, Water Polo, Fives (Eton), Fives (Rugby), Korfball, Pistol Shooting and Table Tennis. The Women's Matches include Football, Judo, Orienteering and Rugby Football.

Perhaps the concern with games and sports is not quite as great as twenty years ago, when the examination pressures were less, yet it is clear that a huge amount of the time and energy of the students, and of the many senior members who coach and support them, is given to sport. Many English sportsmen developed their skills at university and the first unified 'Cambridge rules' of football were devised here in the middle of the nineteenth century.

Several theories could be put forward to explain this. There is the old adage 'a sound mind in a sound body'. That is to say, if one's body is clean and lean, one's mind will work better. This is certainly part of what drove me out onto wet, cold and muddy fields. This fitness is not just the muscular exercise, which relaxes and tones up the body, but the relaxation of the mind.

In a university, one is under constant mental pressure, writing the next essay in one's dreams and all waking hours. Something rather powerful is needed to clear the mind. The Japanese have Zen and the tea ceremony. Alcohol or chess can help. Rowing along a misty river in perfect unison

---

3   http://www.theboatrace.org/origins

early in the morning as the sun rises over the willow trees or being involved in executing complex moves in a game of football or rugby has a similar effect. It is difficult to think of a problem in physics or history in the midst of a rugby scrum.

I was told at school that games were important because they taught me lessons for life. Team games both expressed and gave instruction in three things which would stand me in good stead well beyond the particular game. The first was that while the action was proceeding in its bounded arena, the game was all that mattered. I should play as hard as possible, try to win, struggle and strive. Yet, in the end it is the journey, not the outcome, that matters. I was to learn that whatever the game, including larger games like local or national politics or any other competitive situation in life, I should remember that a game is only a game. A good loser was as admirable as a good winner.

The second lesson is that we have to play by the rules. Rules are general and minimal and the art is to steer as close to their edge as possible, without breaking them. One should pass the ball *almost* forwards, tackle with energy and skill but *not* trip up deliberately, sail, literally and metaphorically as close to the wind as possible. Yet one should never cheat, even if no one could see. Victory by cheating is pointless for you were entrusted to play the game by the rules.

This lesson should apply if you became a lawyer, a politician, a civil servant, a churchman, a banker, an academic or any other professional. Most behaviour is partly competitive and much of it occurs out of sight and cannot be scrutinized. Others trust you to play cleanly. On the playing fields and games courts which surround Cambridge, people learn, as they had to at school, that cheating does not pay, not because you may be penalized, but because you lose your own self-esteem and this subverts the whole point of the game.

The third lesson was that team games improved teamwork skills. It has often been noticed that most of the world team games – including cricket, football, and rugby – were developed in England. And at the heart of these activities, as with rowing, playing in an orchestra or singing in a choir, it is the general good, the team's success, that matters.

The art is to achieve a balance between individual initiative and effort - pulling the oar, dribbling the ball - and the needs of the larger whole. To pull too strongly, to hold onto the ball too long, can destroy the team effort. The activity is largely about collaboration, about depending on others and others depending on you. Thus 'a good team player' is one of the higher forms of praise for a member of a College or Department.

The inter-College and inter-University rivalries are a perfect setting for team sports as 'Houses' were at school. It may not be true that the battle of Waterloo was won on the playing fields of Eton, yet it is clear that if suddenly all sports and games were banned in universities a great deal of the meaning and sparkle would be lost, and the role of these institutions would be diminished. Games are not just a luxury; they are part of the fabric.

Food and drink

Along with the Chapel, the largest and most splendid buildings in the Colleges is the dining hall. Cleanliness may come close to godliness, but it could also be said that consumption is close to devotion. Solidarity is promoted by eating together, as it was in monastic institutions.

The Fellows and the students dine together (i.e. at the same tables, not simply in Hall) to mark the arrival in College of a new 'year' and its departure nine terms later. A new custom in King's and many other Colleges is the 'Half-way Hall' dinner to which students in the midst of their nine terms are invited and are joined by Fellows. In King's, at one of the special feasts at which some of the students are present, a Fellow is asked to give a humorous and perhaps nostalgic account of the history and culture of the College. This binds Fellows and students together for a moment of shared laughter. The King's College Choir sings at some of the dinners, for example that for Founder's Day and Founder's Obit, uniting the guests in another form of contemplation.

Previously, with a small Fellowship, one would have known other Fellows well. Now, in my College at least, it is too big to have this pleasure, and I find the randomness of having to sit next to strangers somewhat disconcerting. Yet I do understand how eating together is a central expression of 'Fellowship'. From the sacredness of the Holy Communion where believers eat the bread and drink the wine together, through to the rowdiest boat club dinner, the sharing of food expresses a form of unity.

Coffee is a powerful stimulant which can help a tired student or researcher squeeze in some extra effort. Ideas do not keep office hours. It is often late at night that the essay has to be written, the lecture prepared, the computer is free. Then coffee spurs us on. Coffee is obviously a sociable drink and Cambridge has a large number of coffee shops where tourists congregate, or one might entertain a visitor in sociable warmth and shared appreciation of this stimulating and relaxing drink.

Tea is different. It is more associated with 'Englishness', more ritualized in its preparation, serving and drinking. The tea party with colleagues or students is often a more formal experience. It is often associated with food, sandwiches, the 'honey' of Rupert Brooke's poem, the bread or scones toasted by the gas fire in the long Cambridge winters. It is a consoling, relaxing, invigorating and restoring drink.

The mind is like a rubber band. It is stretched to capacity by intense intellectual work, by reading, writing, teaching, and experimenting. Yet it also needs to relax from time to time. The pubs and student bars are one of the main places, alongside games and the arts, where this can occur. After a long day in the computer laboratories or Old Cavendish laboratories, the academics repair to *The Eagle* or *The Bath Inn*.

The huddled charm of a busy bar, the welcome glow of a good ale, all induce the nearest many Cambridge people find to what has been described as the spring of religion – effervescence. The difficulties, blocks, puzzles seem to resolve themselves. The imagination is released to play more intuitively with hypotheses. It is possible to go more directly to one's inner thoughts and hunches. Friendship, real exchange of ideas and emotions can occur.

Then there is wine. Medieval England was not merely an ale country, but deeply involved in the wine world of France. English wool was traded down the Cam and Ouse to France and in return wines from that country, particularly Bordeaux, flowed back. The cellars of the Colleges are famous and often valuable.

There is an old saying, *in vino veritas*, 'in wine – truth', and I have always been intrigued by the different interpretations one can put on this. A good meal and good wine with friends in a College indeed does give one a sense that one can speak truth, be honest, close the gap between the constantly watchful self-control of ordinary life, and one's real feelings. One can tell the truth more directly, and learn truths that would normally be kept hidden. This is not surprising. The synapses of the brain which facilitate our thoughts are chemically altered by stimulants contained in all the drinks I have discussed.

Furthermore, these social drinks are expressive. Much of Cambridge life is about distance and closeness, keeping the freedom of separateness, yet communicating closely with people who become friends. Wine expresses this, just as the wine of Communion expresses closeness and the integration with Christ. The circling of the port after High Table, the dying custom of offering of sherry to visitors and undergraduates, the glass of wine at the end of a seminar or book launch, express and also create closeness. As in all things English, it also expresses class.

The World of Ideas

Formal learning

A CENTRAL ROLE of the College is to teach students, most Colleges having several hundred undergraduates and a smaller number of postgraduates. These students come to study in a range of disciplines - the arts, humanities, social sciences, natural and physical sciences and mathematics. The students are chosen and admitted to the College by the Senior Tutor in consultation with the Fellows in the relevant subjects. The selection is usually made on the basis of interviews, and the results obtained by the candidates in various examinations, some of which are organised by groups of Colleges.

The undergraduates are, if possible, taught by the Fellows of their College in the subject they are studying. The course of study of each student is overseen by a 'Director of Studies', who will arrange for specific teachers. The teachers are known as 'supervisors' (in Oxford tutors), while most lectures and seminars are organised by the University not the College, as are the examinations.

The teaching enterprise also needs a manager: the Senior Tutor. His or her responsibilities include the formulation of the College 'admissions policy', in other words the criteria for the recruitment of undergraduates.

The teaching of graduate students, Master's and Doctoral candidates, is arranged by Departments and Faculties outside the College, though such students also have to be accepted by the College, which oversees their social needs.

Cambridge is an old University living in the modern world and its early origins, like that of other European universities, has given it a special oral flavour. For the first quarter of a millennium after its founding there was no printing in the western world and hence everything had to be transmitted orally or in manuscript (parchment or paper). Most teaching was by verbal transmission from Master to Pupil – through personal apprenticeship one became a Master of Arts. This was done in two main ways, by lecturing and by personal one-to-one teaching.

I will concentrate on the personal supervision system, since this is the unique aspect of Cambridge Colleges. The lectures and seminar teaching are common to all universities. The one to one or one to two teaching of undergraduates is organized by the Colleges and mainly performed by College Fellows.

The current College-based supervision (tutorial) system is a late nineteenth century development, evolving out of an eighteenth-century system of private tuition.[4] 'In 1902 the *Student's Handbook* announced that there was 'no need for most students to seek private tuition, as College, intercollegiate and professorial teaching were quite sufficient.'[5] The best College teachers, borrowing from the best tutors, revived the system of question and answer which had dated from medieval times.

Supervisions occur about once a week during full term. Usually each student or pair of students is given four to six supervisions per paper. The student prepares some work, an essay or equivalent. The supervisor has set the topic and proceeds to ask questions and make comments. It can be highly rewarding and exciting, or, sometimes, less than helpful and even embarrassing.

Many of my best ideas have been worked out with students, yet both the supervisions themselves and often the reading of the essays before and afterwards take a great deal of effort. As Rose and Ziman note, 'to be successful a tutorial usually demands a constant and very carefully controlled projection of personality on the part of a supervisor. It requires great expenditure of nervous energy...'[6] The teaching requires a mixture of criticism and confidence boosting. Arthur Benson noted that 'I realized... that generous and simple praise, outspoken encouragement, admiration, directness, could win victories that no amount of strictness or repression could win. I began to see that enthusiasm and interest were the contagious things...'[7]

The effects of this approach are described by the musician Raymond Leppard when writing of his tutor. 'As a teacher, he had that greatest gift

---

4   The changes are well described in Sheldon Rothblatt, *The Revolution of the Dons* (Cambridge, 1968), 207ff

5   Rothblatt, *Revolution*, 234

6   Rose and Ziman, *Camford Observed*, 153

7   Benson, *College Window*, 132

of all of making you feel that he thought you so much better than you knew you were; and you loved him, so you couldn't let him down by not being so.'[8]

Many people get a great deal out of the supervisions as they learn to argue and to sift evidence, 'They learn to discuss intellectual topics freely, fairly and penetratingly. Weekly contact with an older person who is sympathetic yet not too intimate eases them into the problems and perturbations of the adult world.'[9] What is the essence of a good supervision, the teacher who encourages and uplifts the student to do even better, the humour combined with severity, the Master-Apprentice relationship,

The methods vary from supervisor to supervisor, but at the heart of it is an intellectual game, like tennis, where each side plays with arguments and facts. The student through encouragement and criticism gradually grows to understand things at a deeper level.

Informal learning

The supervisions are structured conversations. They fit in with the innumerable conversations which take place in the College. King's is full of talk, along the many paths and through the various courts, research and even more so in the private and public spaces where a ceaseless discussion of issues from the trivial to the sublime never stops. One King's Nobel Prize winner, Sydney Brenner, for example described how it was through almost ceaseless conversation with Francis Crick that they worked out the implications of the discovery of DNA. At meals, after meals, in endless meetings and teachings, formally and informally, the art of conversation flourishes.

The philosopher Michael Oakeshott made the 'conversational' metaphor one of the centres of his thought. He used it as 'an all-encompassing metaphor for the ideal structure of education, social life generally, politics and much else. The traditional liberal University, in which different disciplines are brought together, not in a common substantive enquiry, but in a common *spirit* of enquiry, which involves no sacrifice of any of their autonomy… universities, friendships, clubs, fraternities and the common life pursued within them are, like love and art, as pointless and

8   In Hayman (ed.) *My Cambridge*, 106
9   Rose and Ziman, *Camford Observed*, 70

inconclusive as conversation… simply ends in themselves…'[10]

Virginia Woolf, a friend of several King's Fellows, paints a picture of one of the many such conversationalists, Sopwith of Trinity, who every evening 'went on talking. Talking, talking, talking – as if everything could be talked – the soul itself slipped through lips in thin silver disks which dissolve in young men's minds like silver, like moonlight. Oh, far away they'd remember it, and deep in dullness gaze back on it, and come to refresh themselves again…'[11] All this is obvious, but needs stressing, for it is often thought that ideas are principally worked out by lone academics sitting silently at their desks or in libraries.

Research

The College is an active place for research in almost all subjects. From undergraduate dissertations and vacation projects, through Master's dissertations, to Ph.D. students in the College, the student body is very actively engaged in many kinds of research. Likewise, the Fellows are all expected to do research, whether full time, like the many Research Fellows, or whenever they can make the time away from teaching and administration among the other Fellows.

Research according to the definitions given to research students consists of the finding of new facts, or of new connections between hitherto known facts. In essence it is a pursuit of knowledge which will add to the sum of what is already known. It cannot just consist of the re-arrangement of previously established information - which makes it rather different from the traditions in many parts of the world.

Much of the research in King's is important because it goes well beyond the minimum threshold of micro discoveries, the filling in gaps in a system. It often moves to the much higher level of macro discoveries, changing the paradigms or rules of a discipline and thereby changing our world.

There was also an active Research Centre in the College, set up by Noel Annan in the late 1960's and the home to many influential research projects in the past. Research Managers, an inheritance from that period, are still active in encouraging conferences, seminars and joint projects. One of the marked features of King's, as it is of Cambridge generally, is

---

10   Summarized by Robert Grant in Mason, *Cambridge Minds*, 230
11   Virginia Woolf, *Jacob's Room* (1922, 2004), 39

that no strong divide is made between teaching and research. Both infuse the other and part of the excitement of the College comes from this dual intellectual activity.

The Culture of King's

Religion

KING'S LIKE THE other early Colleges was set up on an analogy with monasteries. Only those prepared to be members of the Christian church could become Fellows. For many centuries only those who would subscribe to the established church could be undergraduates. The current King's Fellowship admission oath to maintain the place as one of 'religion' makes sense in this context.

The generally Puritan tone of Cambridge, certainly from the sixteenth century, suffuses the place so that it is 'lower' church than Oxford. There was no high church 'Oxford movement' here. Cambridge is Anglican, but tolerant. It is catholic with a small c, that is open to many interpretations. This does not mean that religion was not taken seriously. Cambridge was the hub of the English Reformation.

Since then, the stridency has diminished and what I have observed is a form of gently understated, private, Christianity. It is more to do with good manners, the beauty of holiness, respect for order, the acceptance that there are mysteries we have not yet fathomed, rather than a burning fundamentalist zeal. Compulsory chapel went on at King's until abolished in 1912 (and some colleges abolished this long after King's). So there was, as elsewhere in England, conformist attendance, but it was not zealous: 'they go to Church on Sunday, just as regularly as they dress every day for dinner; and regard a man who neglects church, just in the same light as one who eats fish with a knife.'[12]

For many there is a sort of suspended judgement on the whole matter. There may be a God, and like Pascal's wager it may be sensible to err on the safe side and act as if there is one (which is also good for morality and social order), but the actual doctrines, dogma and beliefs are left vague.

If enthusiasm and ardent adherence is a measure of religious sensibility, then for most people there are more important 'religions' in Cambridge than what happens in the chapels. Many are more excited about other passions – rowing, rugby, drama, music, writing, experimenting, drinking,

---

12   Prince Puckler-Muskau in Wilson (ed.), *Strange Island*, 176.

eating – than about the services they attend.

Religion is not banned as a topic of conversation at King's High Table, as it used to be (as divisive) in Oxford. Yet I have seldom discussed it, except in an abstract, distanced, academic way in relation to some particular current event or talk. So, when the Chapel was visited by the Dalai Lama, or used for African drumming or Indian sitar playing, or as the venue for the first public lecture by the ex-Kingsman Salman Rushdie after the fatwa was laid on him, there seems no incongruity or dissonance.

Ritual

There is a large amount of formal, ceremonial, behaviour in Cambridge and in particular in the Colleges. Using the looser definition of 'ritual' suggested by the late anthropological Provost of King's, Sir Edmund Leach, that it is 'standardized, repetitive, communicative behaviour', then Cambridge seems unusually full of ritual. Even in other universities, and certainly in most of life, people are not seen occasionally walking around in formal costumes and meals do not start and end with graces.

When I was at the London School of Economics and School of Oriental and African Studies, I do not remember a single formal ritual of any kind. Yet, in King's, small rituals are going on all the time. One possible explanation for this odd ritualization of life is historical. Unlike most universities, which were founded and developed in the period after the Protestant reformation and the industrial revolution, Oxford and Cambridge grew up in a Catholic and agrarian world. During the later Middle Ages there was a fuller ritualization of life. This was only partly brushed away.

Although many institutions invent some ceremonials from nothing, it is clearly easier and more convincing if one can point to many hundred years of this sort of activity. Many in King's experience a feeling of something old and continuous in the formalized movements, costumes and processions. The effect is not ridiculous because of the buildings. Cambridge is a grand stage for public ceremonial.

Yet historical explanations are never complete, because we are forced to ask the question – why bother to maintain the traditions? Rituals are expressive in that they tell people about themselves and their society. They tell people that they are special, that they are changing from one status to another, and that they are all members of one group. In this sense Cambridge ceremonial is clearly expressive.

The traditional prayers and toasts and singing at College feasts, the little events like champagne at the end of exams, the ceremonies surrounding the May Balls, even the highly ritualized boat races, express many things. They tell both the participants and the world about the sense of belonging, of privilege, of being set apart, of movement through the life cycle, of incorporation and separation from the community. Because King's feels itself special and set apart, it clings to the ceremonies and the ceremonies reinforce that set-apartness and special flavour. It reinforces particularism but also shelters and encourages those within its walls to be somewhat more adventurous.

The rituals which take place in the College are the most obvious sign of the distinctive character of the community. In King's College, the 'admission' of a newly elected Fellow is an impressive *rite de passage* where the ceremony takes place in Chapel. He or she grasps the Provost's hand, swears an oath to observe the statutes of the College and 'endeavour to the utmost of my power to promote the interests of the College as a place of education, religion, learning and research' (an oath which does not prevent the election of atheists), after which the Master says: *'Auctoritate mihi commissa, admitto te in socium huius collegii, in nomine Patris et Filii et Spiritus Sancti'*.

Because of the grandeur of its Chapel, the inauguration in King's, with candles, surplices, oaths in Latin, signing of books, introductions to all the Fellows, organ music and a special dinner are at the impressive end of what vaguely feels like an initiation into a special order – the Masons, Templars, Knights of the Round Table – which, of course, it is.

In some more formal Colleges, dinner begins with a Grace in Latin, using a monastic liturgical form (*Oculi omnium in te sperant Domine...*), and the attempt is still made to make dining in Hall into a ritualized occasion. The Fellows and the students all wear gowns. The Fellows sit on their dais like the lord and his family in a medieval hall, and the College silver is displayed on the table. The food has an obvious symbolic value, with a stress on meat with traditional high-status associations such as venison and pheasant. In King's on most nights there is a much shorter grace at the start and end – *Benedictus Benedicat* and then *Benedicto Benedicatur*. Yet at Feasts and special occasions the longer grace is read.

The ceremony of the seasons

It is often thought that one of the main changes in the last couple of hundred years, linked to the rise of industrial societies, is that time has flattened out. It flies like an arrow and never returns to its point of origin, it is progressive and linear. This is in contrast with time in agricultural societies which is thought of as circular, linked to the seasons, to the sowing, growth and harvesting of plants and the movement of herds – a time to plant, a time to weed, a time to reap, then a time to plant again.

One of the curious features of Cambridge University, and within it King's, is that it maintains, within one of the most rationalized and highly technical parts of a society, a circular rhythm. There are four seasons printed in my Cambridge diary. 'Michaelmas' is the late autumn and Christmas, the time of entry of the fresh batch of students and the starting of lectures. It is a time to sow. The 'Lent' Term is the hard slog through the cold spring, the consolidation of teaching. This is the time of vigorous weeding and tending of growing minds. Then there is the 'Easter' Term, that is the spring and early summer. This is the revision and examination season, the rounding off of many courses. It is the harvesting and laying in of the harvest, and the harvest festivals (May Balls, graduations) and the saying good-bye.

Finally there is the Long Vacation, or as it was renamed recently in the diary to cloud the eyes of suspicious accountants, the 'Research Period'. This is the time for family and recovery from a demanding year. It is also the time for deeper research, writing and foreign trips. It is a mixture of preparing the ground, sorting out the seed for new teaching, long-term projects to reshape the whole terrain.

These cycles are mirrored in nature. King's is filled with flowers, lawns and above all trees, so the academic cycle is linked to the movement of the leaves and grasses. The slight haze of green of the willows on the Backs, the first yellow aconites and snowdrops and then the crocuses, bluebells, daffodils, and later the red tulips, all these reflect the growing year. Full summer brings a green luxuriance. This later turns to red and gold and is blown away by the winter gales.

This circular, living, time, alleviates boredom. King's is not a static and stale place, but rather full of movement and an ever-refreshing renewal. Yet also there is the assurance of continuity, of a safe return, of predictability.

Courtesy and manners

King's is to a considerable extent a 'total' institution, a face-to-face, oral, multi-stranded community. One of the problems the inhabitants of such places face is the considerable danger of creating lasting offence.

From the middle of the nineteenth century, until a century or so ago, a person was often elected to a small College of a couple of dozen dons as a bachelor in his early twenties. This young man would henceforth eat, teach, sleep, worship and play within a tiny community. One day, perhaps up to sixty years later, he would die there and become a name on a wall. He would spend three quarters of his life with roughly the same group of people. If you fell out seriously with a Fellow then it would poison the rest of your life.

On the whole, King's is a highly, some would say, overly, courteous place. Small gestures of opening doors, standing up when people come into the room, thanking people for small favours, greeting people warmly, all are accentuated so that people's self-worth is not damaged. Certainly, amongst the older generation, there is an ethic of gentlemanly (or ladylike) good manners which is stressed.

Likewise, on the whole, the most important part of a person's contribution in a University, their ideas, are treated with courtesy. Whatever one may feel about a person's talk, article, interjection or argument, it is best to cloak your feelings with courteous, if mild, enthusiasm. Of course, if this is just a hypocritical and vapid screen it is not always helpful. Yet the art of framing counter-arguments and criticisms in a way which does not create a permanent rift, which challenges the ideas and not the person who put them forward, is well developed.

There are several techniques for doing this. One is the device of the modulated negative. You do not directly say 'No' or 'You are wrong' when faced with something you disagree with, but you concede a little and then express the negative later on. 'Yes, I see what you mean and that is an interesting approach I had not thought of, but....' 'Yes.... But...' is the classic way of saying 'No' or 'I disagree' without giving offence.

In teaching, the equivalent is to start by praising one or two good points in an essay or argument. After that, most criticisms, however harsh, are accepted without too much pain. They may even do some good. A blistering attack from the start will probably be rejected as too damaging to the receiver's self-esteem.

Courtesy is like oil. It prevents a complex and intricately interdependent machine from seizing up, lubricating parts which have to function alongside each other. Courtesy requires constant attention but is essential in a place where it is very easy for familiarity to breed coldness and for hidden negative feelings to become all too obvious.

A special aspect of courtesy is the way of treating strangers or new acquaintances. King's is both static in that there are long-term friendships lasting decades, but it is also open and full of new friendships. Every year a third of the undergraduates and even more of the postgraduates (with the growing number of one-year Master's students) are new. There are also many short and longer-term visitors. I am always meeting new and interesting people at seminars, committees and dinners. The difficulty is that each new meeting may conceal within it a potential for both great benefits and the reverse.

For centuries, many of the Cambridge intake might look like callow young persons, sometimes obnoxious, sometimes lacking much interest in what one is trying to teach them. One day, however, they might well become great poets, statesmen, explorers, television presenters or comedians. Their memories of the place and of you may well be of value in some way. So, it is prudent to treat them with respect. In fact, this applies to everyone. The rather loud-mouthed and ill-informed individual one sat next to at a dinner may turn out to be on the Committee to consider your upgrading or whether the University Press accepts your next book. In this small and inter-connected world. you can never be certain. So, it is sensible to be courteous and pleasant to everyone.

This courtesy is also, in the English way, a device to keep people at a reasonable distance. It is the courtesy of an old-fashioned dance, a certain stiffness and holding at arm's length, which may be relaxed later into intimacy. It is like talking about the weather, a set of rather empty, low-charged gestures and remarks which establish a formal relationship without committing oneself too much.

✳✳✳

Courtesy has to be learnt. Mistakes can be the cause of great embarrassment. When I first came to Cambridge it was courteous to shake hands on greeting both men and women. Now one seldom does so, except to people from abroad. At that time one very seldom kissed a lady friend as a greeting, and never embraced a man. Then, through the eighties, the courtesies changed and now it is a complex art.

Which male friends does one embrace? The old rule that one only did so to people from Latin (and especially South American) countries no longer holds. Is this a student one should kiss? Should one do so on meeting or saying goodbye? Inside one's rooms or publicly on the step as she leaves, on one or both cheeks, touching the cheek or not, with or without an embrace?

A book could be written on just this theme of the courteous greeting and great care has to be taken in a climate of suspected sexual abuse and where many cultures meet. To kiss a Japanese visitor would be a great discourtesy, and even to kiss one's wife in front of a Japanese person is extremely rude.

At the heart of courtesy is a concern for the other. All courtesy is about making an extra effort, by bodily or verbal signals, to show an appreciation for the other, to pay special attention to them as ends and not merely as means. It is very easy to become so involved in one's thoughts, happiness or anxiety, that one forgets the common courtesies. They become covered over by rush, self-regard, and laziness. My grandfather's advice when I was about eight was that however shy, apprehensive or tired I felt, I should enter a room or a relationship with a warm smile and a genuine awareness of the state of the other.

It is also worth noting the difficulty of disentangling oneself from the other, of saying goodbye. I remember as a first-year undergraduate at Oxford being very puzzled as to how to eject talkative friends from my rooms when I wanted to go to bed. I could hardly push them out, or even ask them to leave. I devised a method which worked. I would invite them to stay as long as they liked, but say that I was off to my bedroom to get some sleep.

Students and visitors do not always know how to leave or know when the meeting is over. If it is someone senior and sticky, I sometimes say that while I am delighted that they stay as long as they like, unfortunately

I have an (invented) appointment - so we leave together and I head off round the building and return to my rooms a few minutes later. The art of gauging how time is passing without rudely looking at one's watch or mobile phone is another skill that has to be learnt over time. I have found that it is best not to try to look furtively, but to make the looking very open and explain why one is doing it.

There are numerous new aspects of courtesy. Previously there was the question of how to invite people to meals, how to reciprocate invitations, how to thank people. Now this whole area is increased in complexity by the new etiquette of e-mails and texting. E-mailing is an area where there should be more explicit instruction since the absence of courtesy, or unfamiliarity with the etiquette, can easily hurt people's feelings – and one is unlikely ever to learn this. E-mails appear to be very informal, but I have found that a little extra energy and courtesy, 'Dear X' rather than a bare message, except to close friends and in a quick exchange, combined with a rather formal ending (as in letters – With best wishes, XX) is advisable. A 'thank you' at the start and other little extra signs of attention seem to be appreciated.

The general point is that the small courtesies of everyday life within the total institution of King's are particularly important. It is like an elaborate game or dance where the rules and the etiquette are there for a purpose. If they are ignored it can lead to long-term embarrassment or worse.

Irony

The art of using words carefully to say things which are often the opposite of what you mean has perhaps encouraged the most characteristic linguistic feature of Cambridge (and the middle-class British in general) – irony. Irony, of course, is a device which a person has to use when direct speech is inhibited in some way, by power, by social distance, by a desire to say something indirectly but effectively. Irony works only if there is a great deal of shared culture between the speaker and listener, so that the slight exaggeration, the mocking tone, or some other signal indicates that the remark has to be turned on its head. If one says of the Provost that he is the best thing since sliced bread, you may mean it – but the look in the eye, the sardonic tone, or the unlikeliness of the comparison may well convey one's real message. This is a culture which has long valued wit and repartee and many jokes and witty sayings are savoured and repeated.

Learning the art of irony is one of the most important skills in Cambridge. It is also important as it is sometimes used to exclude outsiders or newcomers. Many people have never been trained in this art, and indeed, from many parts of the world, see it as a hypocritical, indirect and odious form of speech. It cannot be mastered without getting to know the place, the people, the history and the culture fairly well. Once mastered, it is the salt which savours many an interaction. It also binds people together in a kind of shared intimacy, as with a secret language.

Space and privacy

Another unusual feature of King's is that space seems to be pre-industrial. In the village in Nepal which I have often visited for my anthropological fieldwork, each part of the village and the surrounding fields or forest have different values. It is an inhabited landscape where certain rocks and trees and waterfalls are the abodes of spirits. Other areas are special in other ways, associated with memories and myths. The mix of the sacred and profane is clearly present.

Most people, living in an advanced urban landscape where there are few special spaces, have lost this feeling. It may be temporarily aroused by particular activities; feverish drinking on a Friday evening, a football match, a disco or wedding party. Yet these are only limited moments of created effervescence in a generally spiritually flat and neutral landscape.

King's College has always surprised me because the spaces are so demarcated and charged with different meanings. 'Holy' or 'sacred' is not quite the right word for these, although they are certainly 'set apart' in some way. In Cambridge, each courtyard, laboratory and department, each park or bridge has its special atmosphere and feels different. It feels like a qualitatively differentiated landscape, not quite 'tribal', yet not quite 'modern' either. It is a mysterious place where memories, values, feelings seem entwined and enriched in a way which I certainly do not feel as I wander through most universities or cities elsewhere. It has an almost magical feeling of otherness, which it is impossible to pin down yet which many sense.

Shutting yourself off is a feature which is widespread in Cambridge and indeed one of its most marked features. I taught for over thirty years in an inner room in King's College and there was a series of seven doors between the outside world and myself. There were the College gates; the outer door to the staircase, the 'oak' or huge outer door which, if closed, means that no-one can disturb me; a thin baize-covered door for notices; the actual door to the outer room; a first and second door on the tiny passageway into the inner room. Instead of the number of telephones or thickness of the carpet denoting status, one's position in the academic hierarchy seems to be measured by the number of barriers a person can place between themselves and the outside world.

In that innermost sanctum, I could work in my private space, or I can invite in particular students and colleagues for the intimacy of something which vaguely reminds me of a Japanese tea ceremony. In Japan, the effect of the tea ceremony is best created by moving into timeless contemplation by crawling through a very narrow entrance, after having walked along a specially contrived 'dewy path' through rocks and mossy trees.

Students arriving for a supervision in my rooms came along the semi-sacred paths beside the lawn, or perhaps even, if I accompanied them, over the sacred grass itself. They moved through the six doors into a place where I had no telephone, no clock and the computer, a recent intrusion, was switched off. To complete the analogy, I usually offered them a cup of green tea before we began to work.

In this most private of inner spaces, the mind can move on silence, away from the rush and chaos of ordinary life. There is the privacy-with-sociability, a chance for real exchange and equal conversation. It is one of the thousands of quiet pools of thought distributed all over the University, especially in the Colleges.

I did not call this space my 'office', which is something I had in the Department, and that has associations with administration as well as teaching. I called it my 'room'. It was in some sense an extension of my private home. It is this aspect which explains the rather peculiar feel of some of the College rooms I have visited.

My own inner room over the years, and now, in another way, the larger outer room I share, resembles the description which Peter Snow gives of a typical don's room. 'Amongst the artefacts will be evidence of foreign travels – some carved black African horns or Andean figurines. There will also be small but distinguished collections of stains on chairs and carpets commemorating expensive drinks spilt over the decades. Everything looks shabby and used...'[13] As an anthropologist, my rooms have been filled with dozens of artefacts – tiny shoes for bound feet, a headhunter's basket, a shaman's water clock, a Mandarin's finger-nail guard, pots and portraits, and a wide range of green teas. The stains of tea and inexpensive sherry circle the frayed rug from the village in the Himalayas where I did my first fieldwork.

The public and the private, and the levels of the private, the *vous*, *nous*, *tu* and the *moi* as the French put it, are carefully kept apart. This allows the mind to continue its silent toil within the extremely busy and overlapping world of Cambridge. It can lead to a kind of minor isolation, or to a sense of careful respect for other's freedom, depending on how one looks at it. The eccentricity, freedom to think crazy thoughts or behave in unusual ways which is cherished in King's is one fruit of this.

Reserve

It is understandable that when one is pursuing some abstruse topic it is difficult to bring oneself back to what feels like trivial chitchat. After a few remarks about the weather or some national event, what is there to talk about? Lecturing or teaching around a focused subject is fine, but chatting about the latest development in number theory, pre-Socratic philosophy or French structuralist anthropology is not really possible. Any tendency towards introversion can be exacerbated, particularly in the early stages of a career as one pursues a narrow topic for a Ph.D.

It is worth being aware of this streak in King's. Many students and visitors have struggled to keep up an animated conversation with some high-powered academic they have accidentally found themselves sitting next to. They should remember that even that person's colleagues may find that conversation quickly dries up.

It may partly be affected by the Puritan heritage of minimalism and self-control; it may be the stiff, middle class, education, including the punishing effects of early separation from parents and being sent to boarding schools. It may be that certain rather in-turned personalities go with great abilities in intellectual work. Whatever the combination of reasons, it is obvious that the English *sang froid*, cold blood, the feature that can easily be mistaken for haughty arrogance, or a boring lack of emotion, is quite common in Cambridge.

---

13   Peter Snow, *Oxford Observed* (1991), 146

The reserve is also part of the delicacy and consideration that is often displayed. One aim in this 'virtual village' is not to trample on other peoples' personal space, their ideas or their self-esteem. Reserve is also displayed in the well-known tendency to understatement. 'An Englishman understates, avoids the superlative, checks himself in compliments...' and consequently visitors are advised 'Be modest. If you are a world tennis-champion, say, "Yes, I don't play too badly." If you have crossed the Atlantic alone in a small boat, say, "I do a little sailing".'[14]

The reserve is shown in many other ways. The normal costume of a Cambridge don, as I have known it, is usually nondescript and informal, though the patched, tweed jacket, dull tie and corduroy trousers have now given way to open shirt, crumpled jersey and jeans. The older and more tattered the gown worn on formal occasions the better, and many shoes are scuffed and unbrushed.

I cannot recall ever seeing a colleague cry, wave his arms wildly or use other forceful body language in normal life. Games and rowing, of course, are different and all the reserve is lifted and a person is transformed into a yelling, waving, excited animal – the release is presumably one of its attractions.

This cautious humility also makes collaborative academic life easier. In order to play the team game of the pursuit of knowledge, each player must know his or her limits. If a Nobel Prize winner in physics thinks he can thereby pontificate on medieval history, he or she will soon be gently put down.

The rapid advances in theory and data about the world means that only by an extreme division of intellectual labour, whereby each person focuses on a small part, can understanding be advanced. To be aware of what we do not know is an essential prerequisite. When a person does speak, his or her words have added value because they have not debased the currency by asserting a certainty in fields where they only have a superficial background.

---

14   Ralph Waldo Emerson, *English Traits* (Boston, 1884), 93; Maurois in Wilson (ed), *Strange Island*, 260.

King's and Eternity

The cycle of observances as the years roll by gives insiders in King's the comforting impression that nothing is changing. In fact, there is a general awareness that everything is changing, and more specifically that the distinctive characteristics of the College are gradually being eroded under pressure from the outside world. The space of most Cambridge Colleges remains inviolate, with the public admitted only when the College allows it, but the traditional rhythm of the year has become harder to preserve, since the staff are oriented towards weekends and Bank Holidays rather than University Vacations.

Most students do not realize it was ever different, and their lives are dominated by their own three or four-year rhythm. As for the Fellows, their attitudes illustrate the importance of the past in the present. 'Of course, twenty years is not very long in the life of the College' my friend Peter Burke heard one of the older Fellows remarking at lunch in Emmanuel College. 'When a College has survived the Black Death' (as a colleague from an older foundation puts it), 'it learns to put other problems in perspective'. Awareness of the past, expressed in the rules of seniority and the rituals of commemoration, the visits of the older Old Members and the way in which some Fellows who died ten or twenty years ago recur in the conversations of the people who knew them, seems to go with confidence in the future.

King's was founded in 1441. It will soon celebrate its 580th anniversary. The 500th anniversary of the completion of the body of the Chapel occurred in 2015. The changes in the world during that half millennium have been amazing. King Henry VI coming back to the College he so meticulously planned would be startled at what he would see. Yet as he dug deeper, he would also be impressed that while the game has changed immensely, it is still in essence the same game. The communal pursuit of excellence in 'education, religion, learning and research', as the Fellows still promise in their oath, is unchanged.

Somehow, in the midst of a modern city and civilisation, King's has preserved a parallel world of customs and community which is unique. This preservation is far more difficult than just preserving old buildings, and far more worthwhile. I hope you will enjoy your time participating in this ancient experiment, and in exploring this extraordinary, ever changing, yet constant College, with its great tangible and intangible heritage.

Some King's people

PREVIOUS CHAPTERS HAVE described some of the institutional and cultural features of King's. This only gives a little of the picture. It is through examining the people who are associated with a College over its long history that we will get a deeper insight into its nature. I will touch on this briefly since others have given a fuller account of members of the King's community.

There is a danger of giving a seriously outdated impression of the culture of King's, especially if one is an elderly retired Fellow. Much of the material presented here concerns a period up to the 1970s when I first arrived. In the almost half century in which I have been in the College, King's has both stayed basically the same but also changed enormously.

The admission of women as students in 1972, a year after I arrived, has transformed the College. For the last few years, women students have constituted around half of the intake of the College. Yet largely because they arrived relatively recently as Fellows, only 30 of the 120 or so Fellows are currently women. Everything about the College has been altered by this change and I noticed straight away an increase in the quality of the life in the College.

Women excel in every way and many of Kingswomen, including Zadie Smith, Lily Cole, Bridget Strevens Marzo, Tamasin Day-Lewis, Judith Dunn, Anne Glover, Philippa Levine have gone on to distinguish themselves. Many notable Fellows and Honorary Fellows such as Caroline Humphrey, Judith Weir, Anne McLaren, Caroline Elam and Lisa Jardine have added distinction to the College.

When I came to King's, the intake of state and privately educated students was still skewed towards private schools. King's now has more than two thirds of its students coming from state-funded schools. When I came to King's almost all of the students, and most of the Fellows, were from British backgrounds. Now many of the students and staff come from all over the world, many from Europe and America, and an increasing number from the Far East, especially China.

The College has changed for other reasons. The number of students has increased modestly as has the number of Fellows in all categories. Yet the turnover of Fellows has increased to such an extent that a situation which I remember when I came to the College, where all the Fellowship more or less knew the names and faces of the others, has changed. It is really only among the older Fellows, particularly the much increased group of retired Life Fellows, that it remains a face-to-face community, as well as younger research fellows who ae often in college because they live there.

Technological changes, in particular the use of computers, the internet and social media and smart phones, all have changed the nature of studying and learning greatly. The College, Faculty and University libraries are now largely a quiet place in which to use electronic devices to search for materials on-line. The connections between students and their family and friends at home are more intense and continuous than when I was at University or even when I came to King's. Meanwhile the social contacts between the Fellows and students, for which King's was famous, have tended to be eroded, particularly because of the increasing work pressures on all those in the College.

There are new buildings, including hostels, but in this respect King's has changed less than a number of Colleges, which have filled out their grounds with new buildings. Much of the architecture and the open spaces at King's have been preserved and embellished, rather than engaging on extensive new buildings. The facts that the student body has not increased greatly, and the College has not had an economic boom, unlike a number of other Colleges, and has consciously pursued a policy of keeping its beautiful buildings unspoilt by modern additions, means that the physical landscape has changed less than in many other Cambridge colleges.

Those who visit, or plan to study at King's, should not take away from this book a picture of an old museum filled with dusty portraits. The vibrant and ever-changing and global institution it now is can be seen on the various College web-sites.

For those interested in learning more about the people asocated with King's, there are the two excellent volumes by Patrick Wilkinson taking the story up to 1973. Wilkinson was a classical scholar, Senior Tutor and Vice-Provost of the College, and long-time obituarist. On the basis of his deep knowledge, he composed two detailed volumes describing those who had been associated with the College between 1873 (when the first non-Etonian Fellow and Scholar were elected in modern times according to Wilkinson, though the first non-Etonian Scholars were in the College by 1865) and 1972 (when the first woman students entered the College).

Comprising more than five hundred pages, *A Century of King's, 1873-1972* (1980) and *Kingsmen of a Century, 1873-1972* (1980) are amusing and deeply informative. *Kingsmen* describes some 1300 people associated with King's, arranged under twenty-nine spheres of activity. Statistical appendices give figures on the educational background of those who came to the College and the careers they followed afterwards.

For the period since 1973, Karl Sabbagh edited a lavish volume of memories, analyses and photographs in his *A book of King's* (2010), with over forty contributors who described all aspects of the College in what can be seen as an oral modern history.

Another insight into King's alumni is provided by the 895 biographies of people who have been described on *Wikipedia,* listed with links at:
https://en.wikipedia.org/wiki/Category:Alumni_of_King%27s_College,_Cambridge

Another insight into King's people is provided by a set of interviews which I have carried out since 1983 and uploaded to the Streaming Media Service of the University of Cambridge and Youtube. The series has now reached more than 240 in total, about one sixth of whom are associated with King's.

The aim of the (on average) two-hour filmed interviews is to discover as much as possible about the family background, early life and schooling of an individual. This is to help us understand the later creative and intellectual activity of the subjects of the interviews. So there is a good deal about King's and its ambience in a number of the interviews. Detailed summaries accompanying the interviews, which can be searched for references to King's, make it easier to locate what was said about the College.

The atmosphere of the College described in the interviews, particularly in those of some of the older Fellows such as Peter Avery, David Willcocks and Patrick Bateson, give rare glimpses of a former age. The series continues up to the present, and recently included films of two widows of Fellows and the Senior Horticulturalist.

Details of these interviews are included in the Appendix at the end.

Films set in King's

During the summer of 2009, as I retired from over thirty-four years of teaching in the University and finished my book *Reflections on Cambridge*, I was visited by a former Master's student, the distinguished Chinese documentary film-maker Xu Bei. Bei suggested I walked round King's College and the University and explained various features of both to her, on camera. We did this and the 29 films set in King's are on the Streaming Media Service at:

https://sms.cam.ac.uk/collection/2745716

There is also a training film, 'Fragments of Kings' made in 1984 by a former Ph.D. student, Sofka Zinovieff, at: https://sms.cam.ac.uk/media/1402102. This shows how much the College has changed even in the last 34 years.

A number of films, including that of the novel 'Maurice' by E.M. Forster were partly filmed in the College.

The particular character of King's people

At the end of his mammoth project, Patrick Wilkinson summarized his impressions of King's up to 1980.

> Kingsmen in general have a tendency to be suspicious of authority and not to accept orthodox opinion unquestioned. E. M. Forster is an extreme example. They are independent and orginal, and often in advance of their times. They are tolerant. Their views are what are broadly known as 'liberal', whatever way they may vote in elections. They tend not to be ambitious in a worldly way. .... Most tend to be individualists, 'cultivating their own garden' and exerting influence, if they do, by writing. Their interests are chiefly of the kind known as 'cultural'... Music has particularly sustained them...
>
> (*Kingsmen*, pp.372-3)

This catches some of the spirit of King's but necessarily omits a great deal, particularly for the period before 1873 and after 1972. Looking over the whole the history of the College I will add a few further general thoughts.

The College has produced some important statesmen - two of them are described below. It has produced some important scientists and mathematicians. It has had influences well outside Britain, in particular in relation to India and China. It has attracted a number of important non-conformist families, including the Rowntrees, Frys and Sainsburys. It has produced a number of thinkers concerned with international peace and reconciliation.

The College is also notable for members who have produced a number of inventions that have changed the world. These include the water closet (WC), the slide rule, the use of fodder crops for over-wintering animals and the electronic computer. It has been especially notable in the twentieth century in the fields of music, computing, economics, anthropology and molecular biology.

One final thing that has struck me forcefully, both in writing this account and in my interviews, is the way in which many of those I have investigated combined excellence in more than one field, often uniting the academic with the practical. Their job, as they saw it, was not just to understand the world but also to change it.

This started at the beginning of the sixteenth century with Robert Lupton, who was a lawyer in the court of Chancery and also a chaplain to two English Kings. He started a boarding school in Yorkshire and was also a notable Provost of Eton. Sir John Harrington towards the end of the same century was not only a classical scholar and translator, but also invented the water closet. In the eighteenth century Lord Townshend was not only an important Whig politician but one of the co-instigators of the Agricultural Revolution.

Moving to the twentieth century, M. R. James was a great medieval scholar, Provost of King's and Eton, but also a world-renowned writer of ghost stories. Goldsworthy Lowes Dickinson was not just a writer and political economist, but also helped to name and found the League of Nations. John Maynard Keynes was one of the great economists of modern times but also started the Arts Theatre and was a major patron of the arts and literature.

Philip Noel-Baker was the only person who has ever won an Olympic (silver) medal and also a Nobel (Peace) prize. Alan Turing was a key figure in the development of artificial intelligence and computer science and also designed code-breaking computers. At the end of his life he was making breakthroughs in in biology. Dadie Rylands was not only an important literary scholar but trained many of the great Shakespearian actors of the twentieth century. Gabriel Horn was an important biologist and zoologist and also a major figure in expanding the science faculties and laboratories of Cambridge.

The list could go on, illustrating the wide-range curiosity and creativity, the confidence and quirkiness, of many of those who have been associated with the College. Those associated with King's have combined serious intellectual work with playfulness and inventiveness. I have found that my friends in the College realize that the divides between thinking and doing, between the sciences and the arts, and between the old and the young are artificial and can be broken down.

Finally, it is worth noting another feature, particularly applying to the period between the later nineteenth century and the Second World War, specifically the Bloomsbury group. This is the fact that many of the leading artists and thinkers believed that the head and the heart should not be separated in the pursuit of truth. This is encapsulated in the famous quotation by one of them, E.M. Forster, in *Howard's End*.

> *Only connect! That was the whole of her sermon. Only connect the prose and the passion, and both will be exalted, and human love will be seen at its height. Live in fragments no longer. Only connect, and the beast and the monk, robbed of the isolation that is life to either, will die.*

The forms this union took are well known, included the fact that conversation, both informal and in the famed *Conversazione Society* (or 'The Apostles') to which many of those featured below under Bloomsbury belonged, was so central in King's. (There is a short description of this society and some papers relating to it in King's at: http://www.kings.cam.ac.uk/archive-centre/archive-month/january-2011.html)

The importance of intense friendship and love is also shown by the fact that a number of those described for the same period were either bisexual or gay, including Goldsworthy Lowes Dickinson, E.F. Benson, John Maynard Keynes, Rupert Brooke, Alan Turing and E.M. Forster. This was again pushing against the bounds of orthodoxy in a period when homosexuality was still a crime.

The selection of portraits

In this small selection of portraits, I have limited myself to some of the deceased and still of continuing significance. Yet even so I have had to leave out a number who some might think should be included. Among these, all except the last two described in Wilkinson's *Kingsmen*: Leslie Charteris (author of the 'Saint' detective series), George Santayana (philosopher and writer), John Arden (playwright), Karl Pearson (statistician), Frank Ramsey (mathematician and philosopher), Sir John Clapham (historian), A. C. Pigou (economist), the Lords Kahn and Kaldor (both notable economists and government advisors), Oscar Browning (maverick and reformer), Alfred Lyall (orientialist) Orlando Gibbons (composer) and Edmund Waller (poet).

Here I will just give a flavour of thirty people who have been associated with the College. The first three are the Kings who built up the College and Chapel. Not being members of the College, but well known historically, I have only included a few details of their support for the College.

Some earlier portraits up to the C19

Henry VI (1421-1471)

Henry VI was the founder of the College in 1441 and his statue is placed at the centre of the lawn in the front court. Christopher Morris writes at the start of his *King's College, A Short History* (1989) that 'The King's College of Our Lady and Saint Nicholas had for over five centuries a reputation for peculiarity. This was precisely its Royal Founder's intention, although the peculiarities have changed in character since Henry VI's time. In the first place it was, in 1441, rather peculiar to found a college in Cambridge, which had attracted no patron since the founding of Corpus Christi in 1352 and of Clare Hall in 1359.'

Originally the plan was for quite a modest College, but then the plans were changed and the grand College we see today was initiated. It was, according to Morris, 'a colossal innovation which set a precedent, firing the imaginations of other men and resulting in spacious colleges elsewhere – Trinity, St John's, Christ's and Jesus in Cambridge, Magdalen and Christ Church in Oxford.' The statutes protected the College from the power of neighbouring Bishops and the University. The statutes also ensured a constant stream of well-trained Scholars, who had to come from Eton College also founded by Henry, though Pensioners (a lower level of student) did not have to come from Eton. Sir Thomas Walsingham, for example, was not from Eton. Finally, the the plans for the grand Chapel that finally emerged, and the magnificent grounds, all have given the College its unique history. The College even today owes much of its special character and charm to Henry VI, a memorial to a man reputedly saintly and murdered at a relatively young age.

Henry VII (1457-1509)

There is a statue of Henry VII, who came to the English throne in 1485, on the front of the College. Henry did not actively involve himelf in the College until the last three years of his reign. He came to Cambridge in 1506 and celebrated St. George's Day in King's. He gave £100 and other gifts to the College. Two years later, in the spring of 1508, further work was in full swing and in that summer he made a large contribution of £4,000. Three weeks before his death in 1509 he gave another £5,000 towards the Chapel and instructed his executors to provide, if necessary, further sums sufficient for its completion. By early 1512 the shell was complete and the rest of the work, apart from the windows but including the extraordinary fan-vaulted ceiling, was completed in the next three years. So 1515 is the celebration date for the building of the Chapel.

Henry VIII (1491-1547)

There is a statue of King Henry VIII, donated in the late nineteenth century, on the front of the College. Henry supported the final furnishing of the Chapel. The glazing of the great windows was probably completed by 1531, and the Chapel was being paved in 1536. The rood loft or organ screen and the stalls against it can be dated between 1533 and 1536 from the initials and insignia of Henry VIII and his then wife Anne Boleyn. The stalls north and south of the choir were slightly later. The chapel was thus completed on the very brink of the Reformation.

When Henry started to abolish the monasteries and chantries there was a real threat that the College would be destroyed. Instead, Henry, decided to support, as well as King's, equally grand Colleges in Cambridge (Trinity) and Oxford (Christ Church). One possible influence in changing his mind may be found in the next image.

Roger Lupton (1456-1539/40)

Roger Lupton was born in the parish of Sedbergh in Yorkshire. He is first recorded at Cambridge University in 1479 as a member of King's College. He became a Bachelor of Canon Law at Cambridge in 1484. He was a lawyer in the court of Chancery, and also became Chaplain to Henry VII and Henry VIII.

Lupton was a Fellow of King's and then became Provost of Eton 1503/4-1535. Lupton Tower, a bell tower built during his time as Provost of Eton, is named after him. He founded Sedbergh School in 1525 as a chantry school, and it became a well-known northern boarding school with strong connections to Cambridge.

As well as being Chaplain to Henry VII and VIII, Lupton was one of the executors of Henry VII's will, with its provision that the Chapel be finished. It is interesting to speculate as to whether Henry VII's late munificence had anything to do with the advice of his Chaplain and one of the witnesses to his will. I also wonder whether part of the reason Henry VIII dramatically changed his mind about the abolition of the funding for Cambridge and Oxford, and instead built new colleges, had anything to do with the advice of Lupton, chaplain throughout Henry's life, and himself the founder of a Chantry foundation.

Sir John Harrington (c.1560-1612)

Sᵀ Iohn Harrington
Tranſlator of Arioſto &c

One portrait which is missing in the College is that of one of its most influential and interesting alumni, Sir John Harrington (or Harington). Harrington was a prominent courtier under Queen Elizabeth (he was Elizabeth's godson) and a scholar, translating Ariosto's *Orlando Furioso* (he was banished from court until he finished his racy translation) and later fell into disfavour again for a satire. He installed the first of a new kind of flushing toilet called an Ajax in his manor at Kelston and wrote a book about it. This makes him the father of the water closet (or W.C.)

Sir Francis Walsingham (c.1532-1590)

FRANCISCUS WALSINGHAM Reg. Elis:a Secretis
A.D. 1573. Obiit A.D. 1590.

Francis Walsingham was at King's College 1548-1550 and his portrait hangs in the College dining hall. He was an important Elizabethan politician and civil servant. Walsingham was principal secretary to Queen Elizabeth I from 1573 until his death. He oversaw much of the foreign, domestic and religious policy of Elizabeth's government, and supported exploration, colonization and the plantation of Ireland. He was important in bringing Scotland and England together and oversaw the gathering of intelligence which helped to disrupt foreign threats from Spain and elsewhere. For this, he is popularly remembered as Elizabeth's 'spymaster'.

William Oughtred (1574 -1660)

GULIELMUS OUGHTRED *Anglus* ex
Academia *Cantabrigienfi* An.° Ætat.73. 1646.

E. S. *fculp*

William Oughtred was educated at Eton and King's, where he became a Fellow. He left the University of Cambridge about 1603 to become an Anglican clergyman. He was rector of Albury for fifty years. After John Napier had invented logarithms and Edmund Gunter had created the logarithmic scales, Oughtred was the first to use two such scales sliding past one another to perform direct multiplication and division. He is thus believed to be the inventor of the slide rule in about 1622.

Oughtred also introduced the 'x' sign for multiplication as well as the abbreviations 'sin' and 'cos' for the sine and cosine functions.

Robert Walpole, 1st Earl of Orford (1676-1745)

Sir Robert Walpole was educated at Eton and came to King's in 1696, but left in 1698 when his father died. He was the first *de facto* British Prime Minister and holds the record as the longest serving British Prime Minister in history, with an uninterrupted period in power between 1721 and 1742. He was a generous contributor to the building of the Gibbs building next to the Chapel.

Charles Townshend 2nd Viscount (1674-1783)

Charles Townshend, brother-in-law of Sir Robert Walpole was a Whig statesman and agriculturalist, educated at Eton and King's. He served for a decade as Secretary of State for the Northern Department and directed British foreign policy.

Townshend promoted the adoption of the Norfolk four-course system, involving the rotation of turnips, barley, clover, and wheat crops and was an advocate of the growing of turnips as a field crop for livestock feed. Hence, he became known as 'Turnip' Townshend and is regarded as a major figure in the British agricultural revolution of the eighteenth century, without which the growing urban population and the first industrial revolution could not have been sustained.

Horace Walpole (1717-1797)

HORATIO WALPOLE, FOURTH EARL OF ORFORD.

Horatio or Horace Walpole, 4th Earl of Orford, son of Sir Robert above, was a Fellow-Commoner at King's. He was an art historian, literary figure, antiquarian and Whig politician. He built Strawberry Hill House in Twickenham in Gothic style and his literary reputation partly rests on his first Gothic novel, *The Castle of Otranto* (1764) and his letters, published recently in 48 volumes.

Rev. Charles Simeon (1759-1836)

Charles Simeon was educated at Eton and King's, which he entered as a student in 1779 and then became a Fellow in 1782. He received the living of Holy Trinity Church, Cambridge in 1783 where he remained for the rest of his life. He is remembered in the simple 'C.S.' on the floor of the Chapel half-way between the North and South doors and lived for many years in the set of rooms above the archway of the Gibbs building. Simeon paid most of the cost of the bridge which now crosses the Cam and the walkway beyond that.

Simeon was Fellow, Bursar, Dean and Vice Provost, and he is remembered as a Christian evangelical, an inspiration for missionaries, and co-founder of the Church Missionary Society. He also helped found the London Society for Promoting Christianity among the Jews in 1809 and was an adviser to the British East India Company in the choice of chaplains for India. He founded the Simeon Trust, and now Simeon Churches are spread over the country and the trustees have interests in nearly 200 parishes in over 40 dioceses.

The Bloomsbury generation

The 'Bloomsbury Group' refers to a loose set of artists, writers and others who had their chief locus in the Bloomsbury area of London, near the British Museum, but also were strongly connected, among other places, to King's College. They cover the period from the start of the twentieth century up to the death of the last of the group some decades later. Apart from those noted below, principal members were Virginia Woolf and her sister Vanessa Bell (whose son Julian was at King's), Clive Bell, Lytton Strachey and Duncan Grant the painter.

Goldsworthy Lowes Dickinson (1862-1932)

Goldsworthy Lowes Dickinson came up to King's in 1881 and was a Fellow from 1887. He was author of many books including *Letters from John Chinaman* (1900), *An Essay on the Civilisations of India, China and Japan* (1914) and *The European Anarchy* (1916). Dickinson was a pacifist, probably inventor of the term 'The League of Nations' and one of the founding committee of the League's precursor, the Bryce Group. He was the major patron and friend of the Chinese poet Xu Zhimo who came to the College in 1921-22 and is here wearing the hat given to him by Xu, whom he mentored in the room above the Gibbs arch. Dickinson's close friend E.M. Forster (with whom Dickinson travelled to India) wrote his biography. There is a fountain-turned-flowerpot now in Chetwynd Court, a memorial to him, originally in Webb's court.

John Maynard Keynes (1883-1946)

Maynard Keynes came up to King's in 1902 as a student and lived in 'The Drain' (now King's Lane) as an undergraduate. Keynes was a polymath, author of many books, and, among other things one of the architects of the post Second World War economic order at Bretton Woods. His ideas fundamentally changed macroeconomics and the policy of various governments and he is widely known as one of the most important economists of the twentieth century. He was also interested in arts. He founded the Arts Theatre in Cambridge, was an important collector of early printed books and paintings (which he donated to the College), and the most munificent donor to the College since the Founder. Keynes' rooms when a Fellow were P3 (over the south gate) and after he married the Russian ballerina Lydia Lopokova (1892-1981) at 17(a) St Edward's Passage across from King's.

Roger Fry (1866-1934)

Roger Fry came to King's as an undergraduate in 1927 and kept close connections with the College in the years until he became an Honorary Fellow in 1927. Fry was Professor of Fine Art at Cambridge and a prolific painter, living in room J10 when he came to the College again. Fry was one of the major figures in the growing appreciation of Impressionist and Chinese Art in Britain, and a founding member of the artistic and literary circle known as the Bloomsbury Group. His paintings can be found throughout the College and he was a friend and co-patron of the Chinese poet Xu Zhimo.

Xu Zhimo (1897-1931)

Xu Zhimo was a famous Chinese poet and writer, whose poem 'Second Farewell to Cambridge' is learnt by many school children. Xu came to King's in 1921 as an associated scholar and spent his last term in Bodley's court. During his time at King's he turned from political economy to poetry and formed friendships with several Fellows of King's, especially Goldsworthy Lowes Dickinson and Roger Fry. His life and work with the 'Crescent Moon Society' was central to the first opening up of China to western artistic and literary influences during the 1920s. There is a white marble stone and a memorial garden in his memory near the willow tree he immortalized by the King's Bridge.

E.M. Forster (1879-1970)

Morgan Forster was an undergraduate in King's from 1897-1901. Later, when he became an Honorary Fellow from 1945 until his death in 1970, he lived on A staircase in the College, in the set which is now the Graduate Students' rooms. He was an essayist and novelist, writing a number of internationally known books such as *A Passage to India*, *Howard's End* and others. He was a close friend of most of the Bloomsbury group, especially Lowes Dickinson and Roger Fry.

Arthur Waley (1889-1966)

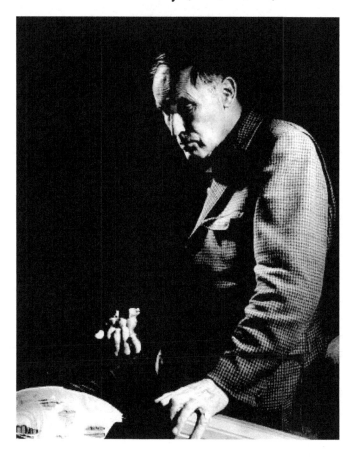

Arthur Waley came to King's as an undergraduate in 1907 and his interest in China was aroused by Lowes Dickinson. He went for twenty years to work in the Far Eastern Department of the British Museum and learnt Chinese and Japanese. Waley was an Honorary Fellow of the College from 1945. Waley translated a number of classic novels and poems of Japan and China, including *The Tale of Genji* from Japanese and much early Chinese poetry in *One Hundred and Seventy Chinese Poems* (1918). He was a mentor of the Chinese writer Xiao Qian (or Hsiao Ch'ien) when Xiao came to King's.

Xiao Qian (Hsiao Ch'ien) (1910-1999)

Xiao Qian spent two years as a research student in King's, 1942-1944, working with 'Dadie' Rylands on English literature. He lived in a room above the present Senior Combination Room in the College. Xiao became a close friend with E.M. Forster and they had a correspondence for some years, parts of it preserved in the College Archive. Xiao was also mentored by Arthur Waley. He later became a famous essayist, editor, journalist and translator between Chinese and English.
The photo was taken while Xiao was at King's.

Yeh Chun Chan (Ye Junjian) (1914-1998)

Near the Fellows' Garden behind the College was the house where Yeh Chun Chan lived 1945-1948 when he came to study at King's at the end of the Second War. He had originally come to King's through friendship with Julian Bell, with whom he had travelled when Bell was a teacher at Wuhan University. Yeh went back to become one of the most important translators of Western writing into Chinese, including the complete works of Hans Christian Anderson (for which he was knighted by the Danish government), as well as writing an autobiographical novel series starting with *The Mountain Village*, chronicling the early years of the Maoist revolution.
The photo was taken while Yeh was at King's.

George Rylands (1902-1999)

George 'Dadie' Rylands was an undergraduate at King's in the 1920s and a Fellow for many years. He was one of the last members of the Bloomsbury Group. He was a literary critic and central figure in the development of drama in Cambridge through the Marlowe Society. In his dining room in the Old Lodge looking out over the back lawn, Virginia Woolf set a dinner party in her novel *A Room of One's Own*. There is a stone inscribed in Latin to Rylands' memory on the ground at the west end of the Gibbs arch.

Some other twentieth century King's figures

M.R. James (1862-1936)

Montague Rhodes James came up to the College as a student from Eton in 1882. He was Provost between 1905 and 1918, living in the Old Provost's Lodge, the next building beyond the library. In 1894 he wrote and published his first ghost story, and it became a custom to invite other Fellows and friends to listen to a ghost story each Christmas. These annual stories were turned into several books, including *Ghost Stories of an Antiquary* (1904), establishing James as one of the world's greatest ghost story writers. He was also an extraordinary medieval scholar and unrivalled cataloguer of early manuscripts. He was Director of the Fitzwilliam Museum, Vice-Chancellor of Cambridge and later Provost of Eton. He was the only person to have been Provost of both King's and Eton.

E.F. Benson (1867-1940)

E.F. Benson, the brother of A.C. Benson Master of Magdalene, and son of an Archbishop of Canterbury, came up as an undergraduate to King's in 1887. He spent part of his time in King's in room E1, where Rupert Brooke later lived. Benson was a prolific writer, publishing over ninety books. Among these were important early ghost stories (*The Luck of the Vails* and others), a series of semi-autobiographical essays on his education, including his time at King's (*David Blaize, David of King's, The Babe, B.A.*) and an amusing account of his contemporaries, including a chapter on King's, in *As We Were: a Victorian Peepshow*. He is now best known for his series of books on *Mapp and Lucia*.

Sri Aurobindo (formerly Ghose) (1872-1950)

Sri Aurobindo came to King's with a classical scholarship in 1890 and gained a first in the first part of the Tripos examinations. He lived in lodgings beside King's (room M2), then known as 'The Drain', where Keynes also later lodged. He returned to India, where he is famous as a mystic, academic, philosopher, writer, critic and political activist (arrested twice by the British). Sri Aurobindo is now remembered in the College by a special tree, planted in his memory, in the Fellows' Garden in 1997 by Sri Chinmoy.

A.V. Hill (1886-1977)

A.V. Hill came to King's as a Fellow from Trinity in 1916. He left Cambridge in 1920 but was elected an Honorary Fellow in 1927. In 1922, Hill was the first British scientist to be awarded a Nobel Prize for Physiology. This was for work related to the production of heat in the muscle, inaugurating the field of 'biophysics'. He married John Maynard Keynes' sister Margaret.

Rupert Brooke (1887-1915)

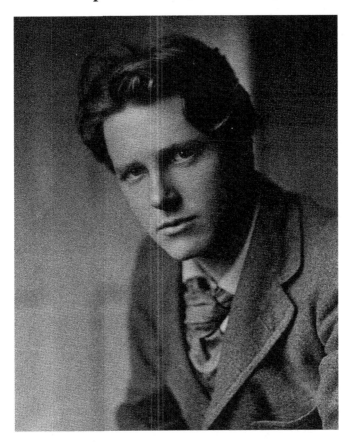

Rupert Brooke came up as a Scholar to King's in 1905 and later became a Fellow. When a Fellow, he lived in room E1 in the Gibbs building. Brooke was a classical scholar and romantic poet whose poems are much loved around the world. His most famous poem, 'The Old Vicarage, Grantchester', with its evocation of the Cambridge countryside, contains lines which are the equivalent in fame for the English to Xu Zhimo's famous lines in his Cambridge poem.

> *Say, is there Beauty yet to find?*
> *And Certainty? and Quiet kind?*
> *Deep meadows yet, for to forget*
> *The lies, and truths, and pain?... oh! yet*
> *Stands the Church clock at ten to three?*
> *And is there honey still for tea?*

Like Xu Zhimo, Brooke died tragically young, while on service in the Aegean in 1915 and was buried on the island of Skyros.

Philip Noel-Baker (1889-1982)

Philip Noel-Baker studied at King's 1908-1912 and was elected a Fellow in 1915. He was a politician, diplomat, academic, outstanding amateur athlete and renowned campaigner for disarmament. He carried the British team flag and won a silver medal at the 1920 Summer Olympics in Antwerp. He received the Nobel Peace Prize in 1959, thus becoming the only person to have won an Olympic medal and receive a Nobel prize. He was a Labour Member of parliament from 1929 to 1931 and from 1936 onwards served in several ministerial offices and the cabinet. He was involved, alongside Lowes Dickinson, in the formation of the League of Nations.

Patrick Blackett (1897-1974)

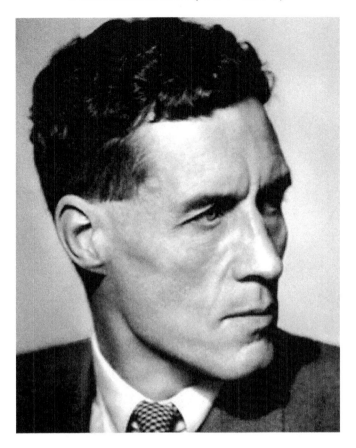

Patrick Blackett came to King's as a Fellow in 1923 from Magdalene College. He was a Fellow for ten years. He was known for his work on cloud chambers, cosmic rays and paleomagnetism, and was a co-discoverer of the positive electron. He won the Nobel Prize for Physics in 1948 and was later president of the Royal Society. He also made a major contribution in World War II, advising on military strategy and developing operational research. His left-wing views also shaped his work on third world development and influenced the Labour Government of the 1960s.

Alan Turing (1912-1954)

Alan Turing came to King's as an undergraduate in 1931 and was elected a Fellow in 1935 at the age of 22. In 1936 he wrote a paper in which he outlined, for the first time, how an electronic computer could be made and Artificial Intelligence could be developed. Later, as a code breaker at Bletchley Park, his work in deciphering the German secret codes (recounted in the film *The Imitation Game*) helped Britain win the war. He also contributed fundamentally to the biological field of morphogenesis. He died in 1954 aged 41.

Patrick White (1912-1990)

Patrick White studied French and German literature at King's 1932-1935. He published twelve novels, three short-story collections and eight plays. His novels include *Voss*, *The Living and the Dead*, *Happy Valley* and *The Tree of Man*. In 1973 he was awarded the Nobel Prize in Literature, the first Australian to have been awarded the prize.

John Richard Nicholas Stone (1913-1991)

Richard Stone was elected to a Professorial Fellowship at King's in 1945. In 1984 he received the Nobel Prize in Economic Sciences for developing an accounting model that could be used to track economic activities on a national and, later, an international, scale. He is sometimes known as the 'father of national income accounting' and was the author of studies of consumer demand statistics, demand modelling and economic growth.

Frederick Sanger (1918-2013)

Fred Sanger was originally at St John's and became a Fellow of King's in 1954. In 1958 he won a Nobel prize for sequencing insulin, and then a second Nobel Prize in 1980 for techniques used in sequencing nucleic acids. He is only the third person to have won two Nobel prizes in science and the only person to have won two prizes in the same subject. The Sanger Centre outside Cambridge is named after him.

APPENDIX: King's Interviews

The following are King's related people in the series of interviews I have made, starting with a series of anthropologists and historians, interviewed because they were in my own fields of expertise.

Anthropologists

Meyer Fortes   Edmund Leach   Ernest Gellner

Jonathan Benthall   Alan Macfarlane   Caroline Humphrey

Stephen Hugh Jones   Jonathan Parry   Piers Vitebski

Stanley Tambiah   Stephen Gudeman   Robert Foley

Historians

Eric Hobsbawm

John Dunn

Mark Elvin

Lisa Jardine

Gareth Stedman Jones

Jean Michel Massing

Biological sciences

Fred Sanger

Patrick Bateson

Gabriel Horn

Hal Dixon

Sydney Brenner

Barry Keverne

Michael Bate

Azim Surani

Charlie Loke

Physical sciences and computing

Dan Brown

John Meurig Thomas

Dan Mackenzie

Ken Moody

Martin Rees

Herbert Huppert

Haroon Ahmed

Hermann Hauser

Keith van Rijsbergen

Others

Peter Avery

David Willcocks

Faith Raven

Wynne Godley

Rosemary Polack

Frank Kermode

Geoffrey Lloyd

Bob Rowthorn

Nicholas Phillips

Neal Ascherson

Leo Sharpston

Stephen Cleobury

Martin Jacques   John Eliot Gardiner   Steven Coghill

Michael Proctor   Mark Smith

These interviews can be seen at:
https://sms.cam.ac.uk/collection/2745645
They are also on my Youtube 'Ayabaya' channel, where they can be searched by name.

APPENDIX Some cultural rules

A few years ago, I began to supervise Ph.D. students who came from far away, and in particular China. I discovered that they found it difficult to adapt to Cambridge. It is an old place with many local customs and cultures which are seldom explained to newcomers. So I wrote down a few simple do's and don'ts for my students.

1. Do not talk about yourself too much, unless specifically asked to do so.
2. Show as much interest as possible in the work of the other.
3. Do not ask personal questions of people until you get to know them.
4. Do not continue to argue or justify yourself when it is clear that the argument is lost – but graciously concede defeat.
5. Try to detach yourself from your arguments so that, if you are criticized or attacked for them, it does not affect you personally.
6. Try to avoid arguments about contentions subjects – politics, religion, sex, etc., until you get to know a person well.
7. Assume that the person you meet is at least as intelligent as you.
8. Assume that the persons you meet are trustworthy – until proved otherwise. The community is based on trust.
9. Do not gossip about other people. Academic circles are small and often highly interconnected and it may easily get back to the persons you talk about. Furthermore, people will not trust you if you are a gossip.
10. English middle-class language is based on the understatement. Hence 'quite good' means 'very good indeed', 'novel' means 'highly original', 'elegant' means beautifully crafted. Hardly ever use 'excellent', very original etc. of your own work.
11. If people make suggestions for books or articles to read, people to contact etc., note them down carefully (which encourages the speaker and may be useful later).

12. If you are shown a kindness (invited to dinner, film etc) a nice postcard (or email) thanking the person is always appreciated.

13. At the start of a new academic experience make as many friends as possible, later deciding which will be deep. Attend as many drinks after talks, meetings etc. as possible. It is easier to prune down than to build up.

14. In seminars try to ask at least one question or make one observation.

15. Do not appear to work too hard, even if you are working very hard indeed.

16. Affectionate teasing is appreciated when a relationship gets deep. Bantering with people, e.g. College Porters etc., is also appreciated especially if there is some structural inequality in the relationship.

17. Gifts are to be used very carefully. If given, they should be light, carefully chosen, and symbolic. There is no need to give teachers and ordinary contacts presents. Preferably gifts should be given after something has occurred – expressive of gratitude – rather than before it has occurred – utilitarian and bordering on corruption.

18. It is acceptable within the academic community to approach strangers directly for advice and comments, though if much work is involved, it is good to sound them out first as to whether they have the time or inclination to help.

19. Usually avoid a direct negative when an assertion is made to you, employing the familiar English device of 'Yes… but…' Which in effect means 'no' in a polite way.

20. If you are puzzled or don't understand things, ask for advice. People may assume you know more than you do, but will usually be very helpful when asked – for anything from how to find places to how to deal with course regulations etc.

21. Edge carefully into friendships. One step at a time. Remember the old joke - you spend your second year shedding the friends you mistakenly made in your first.

APPENDIX.

A few tips on how to avoid work stress and be efficient

Life during the short Full Terms of eight weeks in King's is full of so many attractions and obligations. Should you be playing games, enjoying clubs, talking to friends, preparing essays? Given this pressure, I thought it might be useful to write down some of the tips or tricks I have learnt over the year about how to survive the stress of work and play and enjoy life more. Many students and teachers, for instance in China or Japan, work longer hours, but usually they do not face the constant difficulty of balancing many competing claims to their effort. This starts at school, but becomes worse at University as the student is left more and more in charge of their own time planning. It is not something that is explained to most of those who go to University. Elsewhere I have given some suggestions on time management, which may be useful.[1]

1. For certain tasks (e.g. trying to solve a problem with computers, writing an essay, choosing something to buy) set a time limit. As C. Northcote Parkinson famously showed, "Work expands to fill the time available for its completion". If you allow six hours to pack, it will take six hours. If you allow one hour, it will take one hour.

2. For other tasks, always allow a little more time than you estimate you need. For example, if you are walking through a place you know, a walk which should take ten minutes, allow 15 minutes. If you meet obstructions, or friends, you will not be under anxiety about being late. This also obviously applies to catching buses, trains and planes, car journeys etc. It is an application of the famous Charles Dickens remark in David Copperfield: "Annual income twenty pounds, annual expenditure nineteen [pounds] nineteen [shillings] and six

---

1　These are also laid out at: https://www.sacristy.co.uk/blog/2015/10-easy-ways-to-avoid-work-stress#

[pence], result happiness. Annual income twenty pounds, annual expenditure twenty pounds ought and six, result misery." It is the same with time; just a little too little of it results in anxiety rather than misery.

3. Always try to do a job well, but not perfectly. The last one percent, which hardly improves things, often takes as much time as the first ninety-nine percent. 'The best (or better) is the enemy of the good'. 'Good enough' is good enough. Remember that the 'law of diminishing marginal returns on the further input of labour' applies to many things in life.

4. Many things can be put into an actual or mental 'pending tray'. That is to say, if you are not sure what you should do, or whether something is important, put it in a 'pending tray' and leave it for a while. This applies, for example, to requests for things and to many emails. The curious thing is that by leaving them in this suspended state, about half or more will disappear – they were not things you needed to do.

5. Concentrate and do one thing at a time. A major cause of strain in the internet age and high consumption age is that we are assailed by various messages simultaneously, or we are tempted to enjoy various things at the same time. Humans only have a limited ability to enjoy stimuli. If you want to listen to music, turn off the television; if you want to talk, turn off or ignore your mobile phone; if you want to enjoy reading, do not listen to music and watch television out of the corner of your eye.

6. Remember that Descartes advice: to start with what you know and the certain, and to proceed to the unknown, makes it easier to solve problems. Also his advice that when faced with a difficult problem it is a good idea to divide it into bits and solve them one by one.

7. When you are working on something complex, or trying to relax, keep a piece of paper (or mobile) beside you and when interrupting thoughts come into your mind, just write them down and then you can ignore them and look at them later to see if anything needs doing.

8. Learn to say 'no' to things which will just distract you from what you really feel you want or ought to do. In saying no,

the way to avoid offence is to use the English technique of 'Yes, but…' 'Yes, I am honoured to be asked to chair that particularly committee, but I don't think I would do it well because …. (my heart is not in it, someone else on it would be better, I would rather wait until I understand the job better) or whatever.

9. Relax for at least ten minutes a day through some kind of physical recreation. Simple yoga, which empties the mind and irons out the tensions of the body, and which is a very pleasant thing to do at the end of the day with one's friend or partner, is perfect. . Also try to walk for at least twenty minutes a day - it will improve your health and many of your best thoughts come when walking.

10. Remember we play a long game. We can now live with pleasure and very actively into our 80's. A particular day, month or year is only a part of what is hopefully a long and productive life.

11. Always keep a very small notebook and pencil/pen with you. Our best thoughts, and things we must urgently do and have forgotten, occur to us when we are not expecting them. Jot them down. Many great people from Thomas Hobbes and many great scientists have done this.

12. Set a limit on your work. Now that we have the internet, mobile communications, the internet, social media etc., there is a danger that work will expand to fill all our time. This is especially likely since those around us want to squeeze the most out of us. Make sure you keep blocks of time – the evenings, parts of week-ends, etc. free. Otherwise all your time will be eroded. If people complain, explain that as with physical exercise, if you overstretch yourself, quality as well as enjoyment quickly drops off.

Acknowledgements and thanks

Many of the photographs have been kindly supplied from the College Collection by the Archivist of King's, Patricia McGuire. I thank the Provost and Scholars of King's College, Cambridge, for permission to use them in this publication.

I acknowledge the following copyright photographs:

John Maynard Keynes - Transocean, Berlin
Philip Noel-Baker - Edward Leigh
Montague Rhodes James - Hill and Saunders
Richard Stone - Antony C. Barrington Brown

If any rights have not been acknowledged or mistakes occurred, I will try to rectify them immediately on notification.

I am very grateful to the King's College Archivist, Patricia McGuire, the Fellow Librarian Peter Jones for reading and commenting on a draft of this work.

Glossary of some terms used

Partly based on Frank Stubbings, *Bedders, Bulldogs & Bedells: A Cambridge Glossary* (2005)

Alumnus (plural alumni) - literally 'nursling' or 'foster-child' of an institution, meaning those who have passed through an institution, old members.

Backs - more fully 'The Backs of the Colleges', the grounds behind the central Colleges, Queens', King's, Clare, Trinity Hall, Trinity and St John's.

Bedder - short for bedmaker, a woman employed, part-time, to do domestic residential room in a college.

Buttery - a place where certain food and drinks are dispensed.

Court - a college quadrangle, around which buildings are placed.

Dean - one of the Fellows of the College, in holy orders, responsible for services in the college chapel.

Don - a member of the teaching staff at the University or College.

Domus - literally house; the Domus bursar is in charge of buildings and other physical aspects of the college.

Fellow - senior member of the College, the teachers and administrators.

May Week - the first fortnight of June, when various events occur to mark the end of the teaching year.

Porter - the college porter is the gate-keeper of the college.

Supervisor (Oxford 'Tutor') - the teacher of students in personal supervisions.

Supervision - a teaching session, usually with the teacher and one to three students.

Tripos - a University examination leading to an honours B.A.

Tutor - does not, in Cambridge, denote a teacher, but something nearer to the original Latin, meaning a 'guardian', namely someone who looks after one or more students in their life outside formal instruction.

Vacation - the period between terms, when the University is not in full session.

Further information

Books and articles:

E.F. Benson, *As We Were: A Victorian Peep-Show* (1930), chapter 7

M.R. James, *Eton and King's* (1926)

Rodney Tibbs, *King's College Chapel, Cambridge; The story and the renovation* (1970)

Patrick Wilkinson, *A Century of King's, 1873-1972* (1980)

Patrick Wilkinson, *Kingsmen of a Century, 1873-1972* (1980)

John Saltmarsh, 'King's College' in *A History of the County of Cambridge,* vol III ed. J.O.C. Roach, pp. 376-407 (1967)

Francis Woodman, *The Architectural History of King's College Chapel* (1986)

Christopher Morris, *King's College, A Short History* (1989)

Josephine Warrior and Tim Rawle, *A Guide to King's College Chapel* (1994)

Noel Annan, *The Dons* (2000)

Karl Sabbagh, *A Book of King's* (2010)

Ross Harrison, *Our College Story* (2015)

Zilan Wang, *Xu Zhimo Cambridge and China* (2016)

Zeeman, N., and Massing, J.M., (eds*), King's College Chapel 1515-2015: Art, Music and Religion in Cambridge* (2015)

Web resources:

There are video interviews of 45 Fellows of Kings and alumni at:
https://www.sms.cam.ac.uk/collection/1092396

There are 88 films about King's and Cambridge, in the form of short interviews, at:
https://www.sms.cam.ac.uk/collection/1283730

King's College has an informative website, including a virtual tour at:
http://www.kings.cam.ac.uk

King's shop including other books on King's and its Chapel has a website at:
https://shop.kings.cam.ac.uk

Acknowledgements

I am very grateful to Professor Nicholas Marston, Vice-Provost of King's College and Peter Jones, Fellow Libarian of the College, for their most helpful comments and suggestions on a draft of this work.

I am also very grateful to Patricia McGuire, Archivist of the College, for providing all the images, except those on the front and back covers, used in this book.

They are included with permission of the College and I would like to thank the Provost and Fellows of the College for permission to include them.

Any errors in this text are entirely my own and will be rectified upon notification.

Printed in Great Britain
by Amazon

33187708R00061